DREAM
themes

DREAM
themes

A GUIDE TO UNDERSTANDING YOUR DREAMS

DR FIONA STARR & JONNY ZUCKER

BARNES
&NOBLE
BOOKS
NEW YORK

This edition published by Barnes & Noble, Inc.
by arrangement with MQ Publications Limited

2001 Barnes & Noble Books
Copyright © MQ Publications Limited 2001
Text © Fiona Starr and Jonny Zucker 2001

Design by **Balley Design Associates**

ISBN: 0-7607-2718-X

Printed in China

M 1 0 9 8 7 6 5 4 3 2

Introduction

One night I dreamed I was a butterfly, fluttering hither and thither, content with my lot. Suddenly I awoke and I was Chuang-tzu again. Who am I in reality? A butterfly dreaming that I am Chuang-tzu or Chuang-tzu imagining that he was a butterfly?

CHUANG-TZU (3RD CENTURY B.C.)

SINCE THE BEGINNING OF TIME, HUMAN BEINGS HAVE BEEN FASCINATED BY DREAMS AND THEIR INTERPRETATIONS. THERE IS A RANGE OF COMMON THEMES THAT TEND TO PERMEATE ALL OF OUR DREAMS AND THE SAME BASIC DREAM THEMES OFTEN APPEAR IN DIFFERENT GUISES. WE HAVE DIVIDED THE KEY ISSUES INTO THE FOLLOWING AREAS—CREATIVITY, FAMILY, FEAR, CONFLICT, ANGER, DEATH, JOY & SADNESS, LOVE, SEX, AND CHANGE. IN THIS BOOK WE CONNECT OUTER AND INNER WORLDS TO ILLUMINATE WAKING LIVES.

Dreams in history

There is no single explanation for why we dream. A range of physiological and psychological theories has been put forward to try to help us understand the phenomenon. The earliest dream analysts believed that dreams served as a means of communication with the gods. The Egyptians, Babylonians, and Ancient Hebrews were all fascinated by their dreams and began to record the symbols that appeared. The Ancient Hebrews were some of the first to take account of a person's waking life including occupation, family life, and personal characteristics in interpreting their dreams.

In *The Iliad* by Homer, Zeus, the king of the gods sent a dream message to Agamemnon, the leader of the Greek forces at Troy. The Greeks, like the Egyptians, believed that dreams had the power to heal. In ancient times citizens of Athens would sleep in the temples for weeks in the hope of experiencing a dream that would tell of recovery.

By the fifth century, beliefs about dreams and their meanings began to change. The role of the gods and the supernatural world became less significant. Plato, Aristotle, and Socrates were all interested in the role of the dream and how it affected a person in their waking life. Hippocrates—the founder of modern medicine—used dreams as a diagnostic aid, basing treatments on the dream scenarios of his patients.

Plato believed that a dream scene could influence how a person should lead their physical life. Aristotle believed that dreams were representations of a person's waking life and could be ignited by the human senses. For example, if a person became very hot in the midst of a dream, Aristotle would have suggested that they had been dreaming about fire and heat.

In A.D. 150, the Roman scholar Artemidorus wrote a vast five-volume work called *Oneirocriticon (The Interpretation of Dreams)*. This was perhaps the first dictionary of dream themes. In it he proposed that the foundations of a dream lie within the dreamer's waking worlds. Thus the dreamer's work, social status, physical and mental health should all be considered when interpretations are made. This rule applies today and throughout this book you will need to consider your own context to obtain the best interpretations for your dreams. This book simply provides pointers to understanding.

PREVIOUS PAGE: *John Anster Fitzgerald's portrayal of a woman dreaming,* **The Stuff That Dreams Are Made Of,** *shows many common dream themes, including demons, goblins, animals and spirits.*
RIGHT: *Throughout history dreams and nightmares have been common themes in painting. Here in this 19th century Japanese print the artist Kitagawa Utamaro depicts a child having a nightmare and being comforted by its mother.*

Religious dream themes

The Old Testament is laden with dream scenes and interpretations. One of the best-known is the story of Jacob's son, Joseph. Joseph was said to hold the power of forecasting through his dreams. Joseph's dream analyses were often the cause of much sibling rivalry, not only because of the unique power that Joseph possessed, but also because of the content of the dreams. In many of his dreams Joseph dreamt of himself as the superior brother. The others grew angry with Joseph's seeming arrogance and tried to exile him while convincing Jacob that his favorite son was dead. Joseph's power, however, helped him find his way out of a dangerous situation when he was able to help Pharaoh of Egypt interpret his own dreams.

Jacob's Ladder is another well-known Biblical dream story. Some say that the dream of the ladder resting on earth but leading up to the heavens is a symbol for higher communication between God and humans on earth.

Daniel in the lion's den is a third famous dream story, in which Daniel interprets a dream for Nebuchadnezzar, the King of Babylon. In the dream it was commanded that a great and beautiful tree be cut down, thus leaving all the animals and creatures unprotected. Nebuchadnezzar dreamt that he must be chained to the tree stump that remained. Daniel read the dream for the King and said that despite his power within the kingdom, this dream told of greater powers in heaven—God—and that Nebuchadnezzar must accept God as the ultimate ruler.

Dreams are significant in the development of other religions also. The Prophet Mohammed, the founder of Islam, is said to have learnt about most of the Koran through his dreams. He was also well-known for interpreting the dreams of his disciples.

Buddhism has a long tradition of dream interpretation and many of the legends and stories involve the development of dream scenes. The Buddha's mother is said to have dreamt that a tiny white elephant had entered her womb. Brahmins suggested that this dream predicted the birth of a great ruler.

In Zoroastrianism, dreams are linked to the actual time of year or the month in which they occurred. A dream's place within the monthly cycle will affect the meaning and its interpretations.

Dreams in western psychology

In the Western world the modern study of dreams and their meanings really began with the Austrian psychiatrist, Sigmund Freud (1856–1939) and his Swiss counterpart, Carl Gustav Jung (1875–1961). Their theories lie at the root of all contemporary dream analysis and are referred to at different stages throughout this book. It is difficult to describe the nuances and complexities of each theory within this kind of book, so simplified explanations are put forward here.

FREUD AND DREAMS

Sigmund Freud developed the technique of dream analysis, among others, to connect a person's conscious and unconscious minds. His classic book *The Interpretation of Dreams* (1899) summarized the study of dreams over the centuries, and was highly influential. It was the first work to establish the idea that dreams in themselves were worthy of scientific study. It also addressed questions about what to ask in relation to dream analysis. He believed that the understanding of a patient's dreams could have a significant impact on the treatment of their psychological problems, and that dreams could have a powerful influence on the working of the human mind.

Freud suggested that in dreaming, the mind engages in the act of primary process. That is, the dreamer's unconscious fears or desires are transformed into dream symbols. The secondary process refers to the repression of these impulses and symbols in the conscious waking mind. Freud asserted that many of the unconscious desires that appeared in dreams were based on childhood experiences of the dreamer. He believed that dreams were often a way of expressing erotic or sexual desires, and that many dream symbols were connected to notions of sex and sexuality. At its most simplistic, long objects were thought to refer to the penis and fruits and cavernous objects were connected to female genitalia.

Freud based many of his theories on the concept of the id—our primitive instincts—and the repressed desires of the unconscious mind. These ideas are discussed in more depth throughout this book. In the 1920s many theorists disagreed with Freud. Others believed that dreams were not reflections of our unconscious desires but of our waking lives. On the basis of such criticisms Freud revised his theories and made a distinction between those dreams that were rooted in waking experiences and those that were inspired by the id.

DREAMS

For a short period Jung and Freud worked together on dream analysis, but they quickly parted ways due to academic disagreements. Jung largely agreed with Freud on his thinking that dreams were mainly representations of the dreamer's unconscious mind. However, Jung questioned whether a dream was only the consequence of a person's individual experience. Jung had strong interests in anthropology, world mythology, religion and the occult. He recognized connections between dream symbols and the myths and legends that derived from a shared body of historical and cross-cultural knowledge. From this information and piecing together replicated stories, Jung developed the idea that there must be a "collective unconscious"—an innate store of information associated with the human tendency to organize and think in certain ways, regardless of culture, religion, or country of origin. Jung also developed the notion of "archetype." This could be simply described as an innate idea or pattern embodied in dreams by a single image or symbol. The wicked witch, wise old woman, hero or magician are examples of these archetypes.

Jung analyzed every dream on three levels—the personal, the cultural, and the archetypal. You will also get the most from this book if you work on your dream interpretations within as many contexts as possible to find the best fit for you. Jung believed that the dream could be used to guide people on their journey through life. In this sense he saw them as having almost a religious or spiritual function. Unlike Freud, Jung believed that the dream contained much more than a reflection of repressed desires or wish fulfilment. He believed that the dream could be used as a channel through which the dreamer could experience their higher self or their spiritual self.

Like Freud, however, Jung believed that dreams were highly symbolic and he felt that they should not be taken at face value. He believed that the coded messages imparted in dreams can be understood only when the dreamer is ready to hear them. When we are ready to address the complex layers of meaning, our dreams can help us to develop our personal and psychological lives.

FRITZ PERLS

Fritz Perls (1893-1970) was the founder of Gestalt therapy. He believed that all dream symbols were the reflection of the dreamer's world. He felt that the dreams represented aspects of the dreamer's psychology that may have gone unacknowledged through their waking life. Perls did not agree therefore with Jung's ideas of a collective unconscious and universal archetypes. He also rejected Freud's theory that dreams were exclusively concerned with repressed desires or unconscious wish fulfilment.

For Perls, the dream told of unresolved personal issues or conflicts that have not yet been dealt with in waking life. Perls believed the value in understanding our dreams lies within the exact and unique meanings specific to each dreamer. The personal meaning of each dream symbol would help the dreamer though their emotional journey. If we were to literally adhere to this theory, a book like this would not be possible to write. However, it is probably most useful to take what you can from each of the theorists and use what best fits for you.

Perls's approach differed quite markedly from that of Freud or Jung in that he believed that dreamers were able to conduct their own interpretations and therefore they did not need to rely on an analyst. Perls developed a series of useful role-play exercises to help interpret dream imagery. In these the dreamer can take the part of each dream character or object.

MEDARD BOSS

Medard Boss was one of the founders of existential psychology. This theory contends that people find their own life direction and express themselves and their choices through all aspects of their behavior. In 1958 Boss wrote *The Analysis of Dreams*. In this he argued that dreams are nothing more than a representation of daily life occurrences. Because life has no meaning, Boss concluded that dreams also have no meanings. Therefore, he says that dreams should be taken at face value. Some psychologists agree with Boss's non-symbolic approach and think that dreams serve as a way for our minds to dispose of information that would otherwise clutter our memories with too much emotion and experience. If you go along with this view, then perhaps it is still worth reading on to see if you can be swayed.

Dreams across cultures

Many Eastern thinkers believe that dreams can be used to help a person to take control of their life and thereby enhance their spiritual growth and personal development. Some also believe that a dreamer can actually remain conscious throughout their dream in order to facilitate the control of their journey. They feel that it is this conscious dream control that helps a person gain the greatest spiritual rewards.

Other Eastern thinkers believe that sleeping serves as the preparation for one's own death. So each time we sleep we prepare ourselves for the time when we must die. From this we might deduce that it is important to prepare for sleep and dreaming in the calmest and most comfortable way possible.

Many Native Americans also believe that the dreamer has the power to control the outcome of their dream in some way. They suggest that the dreamer should focus on their pre-dream state to enhance the development of their dream or even try to answer any questions they may have. The dream can help a person decide what decisions they should make or what path they should follow. Some Native Americans believe that in our dreams we can encounter a spiritual guide who can lead us to the right place. This leader can reappear in all of our dreams and can be quite a source of comfort. The concept is not really that dissimilar from Jung's archetype of the wise old man or woman.

In the Malaysian jungle the Senoi people have developed their own kind of dream interpretation. They mainly believe that dreams can be modified while they are actually occurring and that we have the power to turn around our dreams to best suit or needs. Thus if something good happens in our dreams, we should approach and embrace it. If we are faced with danger, we should tackle it to help us move on. Learning to overcome our dream fears can help us to manage fears in our waking lives. Being positive in our dreams can help us to feel positive in our waking lives. In this sense dreaming is a two-way process and just as our world affects our dreams, so do our dreams affect our worlds.

In the Australian Aboriginal tradition the telling of a dream is a shared experience and occurs frequently. For some groups if a dream tells of something forbidden—such as a sexual dream about another person's partner—then something in the dream is expected to intervene to prevent this from happening.

Sleep and dreams

Sleep is such a fundamental part of our lives that we rarely stop to consider how it works. In sleep we abandon consciousness, we abandon control of our movements and thoughts, and we become unaware of our surroundings. If this were to happen in our waking lives we would probably be terrified, yet we go through this process every night and without it we feel run down, stressed, tearful, and may have poor concentration.

Modern sleep analysis began at the turn of the twentieth century when scientists monitored brain waves and general physiological activity while subjects were sleeping. It is now widely agreed that a night of uninterrupted sleep consists of four phases or cycles of sleep. The movement from phase one to phase four takes approximately ninety minutes, so a sleeping person will go through about seven cycles in one night.

In phase one of the cycle we move from wakefulness to sleep. In phase two the beginning of sleep is marked as the sleeper becomes unaware of his environment and surroundings. Phase three consists of the gradual transition into a deeper phase of sleep and phase four marks the deepest level of sleep. In this last phase breathing becomes rhythmical and deep. Heart rate and metabolism drop and the electrical activity of the brain changes. Once phase four is complete, the sleeper moves back up through each of the other phases so that the heart rate increases, metabolism speeds up, and breathing becomes shallower. As a person moves back through the cycle, blood pressure often increases and penile or clitoral erections may then occur. Once at phase one the whole cycle happens again.

REM SLEEP AND DREAMS

The fourth phase of sleep is also known as REM sleep, which stands for rapid eye movement. This describes the darting movements of the eyeballs under the eyelids, which have been observed by scientists in the sleep labs. Although dreams can occur in the other phases, REM marks the onset of deep, vivid, and frequent dreaming. It has been suggested that the movement of the eyeballs happens as the dreamer is observing the events that are actually happening within the dream.

Nathaniel Kleitman, an American physiologist, and his colleagues in 1953 conducted a series of experiments in which they observed subjects sleeping. Their objective was to try and explore a correlation between REM sleep and dreaming. They monitored the levels of electrical activities in the subjects' brain and woke the subjects when these activities were at their highest level. The subjects always reported vivid dreaming at that time. The periods of dreaming and electrical brain activity also corresponded with Rapid Eye Movements. This finding marked the beginning of an intense period of study around sleep and dreaming.

> I can never decide whether my dreams are a result of my thoughts, or my thoughts the result of my dreams. It is very queer. But my dreams make conclusions for me. They decide things finally. I dream a decision.

D.H. LAWRENCE, LETTER TO EDWARD GARNETT, JANUARY 29, 1912

WHAT ARE DREAMS FOR?

Newborn babies spend most of their time sleeping and about half of this time is spent in the REM state. REM has also been observed in birds, reptiles, and other mammals. Experiments have shown that people who are deprived of REM sleep become highly sensitive, lose concentration, and suffer recall memory problems, whereas those deprived of non-REM sleep experienced fewer of these difficulties. Some professionals have suggested that in non-REM sleep the body and mind are resting and regenerating, whereas in REM sleep psychological rather than physical regeneration is taking place.

Despite years of research into sleeping and dreaming, many questions still remain. Are dreams a way to process waking information? Are they a way to get rid of too much information that we absorb in waking life? Do dreams serve as a guide for how to live our lives? Or are they a means of raising unconscious thoughts to our conscious awareness? It seems probable that dreams have a number of interrelated and complex psychological, emotional, and physiological functions and whatever the explanations are, they can be used in a highly individual way to explore aspects of ourselves that we may not yet fully understand.

PART ONE

Themes

CHAPTER 1

Creativity

William Morris wanted for a long time to dream a poem. At last he did and was asked if he could remember it. Only the first line, he said sadly, and it went like this: The moonlight slept on a treacle sea.

R.L. MEGROZ

IN THE COURSE OF MY LIFE I HAVE OFTEN HAD THE SAME DREAM, APPEARING IN DIFFERENT FORMS AT DIFFERENT TIMES, BUT ALWAYS SAYING THE SAME THING, 'SOCRATES, PRACTICE AND CULTIVATE THE ARTS.' IN THE PAST I USED TO THINK THAT IT WAS IMPELLING AND EXHORTING ME TO DO WHAT I WAS ACTUALLY DOING;... THAT IS PRACTICING THE ARTS BECAUSE PHILOSOPHY IS THE GREATEST OF THE ARTS, AND I WAS PRACTICING IT. BUT EVER SINCE MY TRIAL, WHILE THE FESTIVAL OF THE GOD HAS BEEN DELAYING MY EXECUTION, I HAVE FELT THAT PERHAPS IT MIGHT BE THIS POPULAR FORM OF ART THAT THE DREAM INTENDED ME TO PRACTICE, IN WHICH CASE I OUGHT TO PRACTICE IT AND NOT DISOBEY. I THOUGHT IT WOULD BE SAFER NOT TO TAKE MY DEPARTURE BEFORE I HAD CLEARED MY CONSCIENCE BY WRITING POETRY AND OBEYING THE DREAM.

PLATO, PHAEDO, C.380 B.C.

Like dreaming, the process of creativity depends largely on the unconscious. For example, it is common to feel perplexed about some kind of problem or creative project and to put it to the back of your mind for a while, when Eureka! the solution jumps out at you. It is almost as if your unconscious mind has been working it all out without your awareness and then when it hits the right button the solution is raised into consciousness. Dreams work in the very same way. In our sleep while we are unaware of it, the unconscious functions independently, bringing us solutions, dilemmas, and adventures. The amalgamation of dreams with processes of creativity provides interesting and fertile ground for psychic and personal development.

Dreams and the creative arts—literature, film, music, dance—all have the power to engage us emotionally and psychologically as if they were real-life events into which we pour our hearts and souls. In fact dreams and creativity have many aspects in common. Both produce scenes and landscapes that can be as clear and vivid as life itself. An artist or novelist can create a landscape that is so evocative it opens up new mean-ings for us and enriches our world. Our dreams, if we let them, have the same effect. Even those who say that they are not creative or cannot paint are able to have wonderfully vivid dreams in which new territories are revealed for discovery.

Equally in acts of dreaming and creation the author will have no idea of outcomes. That is part of the beauty of both processes. Just as novelists create characters with no idea how they will develop and musicians create whole works from a simple turn of phrase, the dreamer will be taken on a journey with no idea of how it will all end. It is our unconscious that decides the outcome of the dream, whether it will end in tears or in glory, or whether it will stop right at the exciting bit where we have to work out what might have been in our conscious minds.

PREVIOUS PAGE: *Dreams, like the creative arts, including works like Chardin's* **Still Life With Attributes Of The Arts,** *have the power to engage us emotionally and psychologically.*
RIGHT: *Jung believed that the appearance of wise elderly figures in dreams, parodied here in the* **Three Old Men of Gotham Went To Sea,** *acted as guides toward spirituality and truth.*

Creativity in dreams

Both our dreams and our acts of creation have the ability to engage us emotionally. We laugh, cry, and get scared in our dreams just as we do when we read a story, watch a film, or see a play. They seem to satisfy a spiritual need in us: the urge to shape, develop, and transform the world that we see. When we watch children at play we can see how this urge to create and recreate seems to be innate. Children use cardboard boxes as magical time machines and clothes become fantastical costumes for drama. As adults we still have this ability and urge to create but, perhaps because of the commitments and responsibilities that come with adulthood, this need is all too often neglected. However, for some, the power of creation is reignited through the imaginative world of dreams.

Some of the best-known creative artists, novelists, and playwrights acknowledge how their dreams provided a source of inspiration—Charlotte Brontë, Mark Twain, Edgar Allan Poe, Graham Greene, Samuel Taylor Coleridge, Robert Louis Stevenson, William Blake, to name a few. In his memoirs Robert Louis Stevenson described how he used to tell himself a story before he fell asleep in order to work on his dreams for inspiration. He talked about the "little people" who carried on the task of writing during the night. Stevenson's most famous tale *The Strange Case of Dr Jekyll and Mr Hyde* was formulated in this way. Stevenson said that the "little people" who developed stories "upon their lighted theatre" deserved the credit for much of his writing.

Another well-known dream-inspired work is the poem *Kubla Khan* by Samuel Taylor Coleridge. Coleridge was suffering from a severe illness at the time and was prescribed laudanum, a medicine often used in the late 18th century which contained a tincture of opium. After taking this, he dropped asleep while reading a travel book in which were written the words "Here the Kubla Khan commanded a palace to be built." When he awoke the poem describing the Kubla Khan's pleasure building was all in his mind and only needed to be transcribed. Unfortunately, before he had time to complete it he was called upon by a friend. By the time he returned to his writing, the words of the dream had slipped away from his consciousness. He was unable to recapture the exact wording and developed only a fragment of what was originally there. Who knows what he might have left if he been able to fully recall the dream's details?

In Xanadu did Kubla Khan
A stately pleasure-dome decree;
Where Alph, the sacred river ran
Through caverns measureless to man
Down to a sunless sea…

They laugh at our play.
And soon they all say,
Such such were the joys.
When we all girls & boys.
In our youth time were seen,
On the Eechoing Green.

Till the little ones weary
No more can be merry
The sun does descend.
And our sports have an end;
Round the laps of their mothers.
Many sisters and brothers.
Like birds in their nest.
Are ready for rest;
And sport no more seen,
On the darkening Green.

The romantic poet

William Blake was also inspired by dreams. Blake used to illustrate his poems with his own engravings. However, this was proving to be a very expensive form of illustration, and he found himself "intensely thinking by day and dreaming by night" about how to develop a cheaper technique that would produce the desired effect at a lower cost. He dreamt one night of his brother who had actually died, but in this dream appeared to him and passed on the wished-for secret—the process of copper engraving.

Musicians frequently report hearing beautiful melodies in their dreams and using them to create wonderful works in their waking lives. The eighteenth-century Italian composer Tartini wrote a piece called *Trillo del Diavola—Devil's Trill*. He said that this music came to him when he was asleep one night, and he dreamt that the devil visited him and started to play Tartini's own violin in the dream. To his astonishment the tune was beautiful—it "surpassed the wildest flights of my imagination"—and Tartini tried to use it to write his piece when he woke up. As is often the way with our dreams, he was unable to recall the tune exactly but at least he managed to use the foundation of it

to create what he felt was one of his greatest works.

Salvador Dali is perhaps the best-known artist who utilized his own unconscious processes, often emerging through his dream world to create masterpieces. From about 1927 onward, Dali was increasingly drawn to Surrealism. The movement was highly influenced by the psychoanalytic theories of Sigmund Freud (1856–1939), probably the most influential psychologist and analyst of dreams, which were relatively new at that time. Dali worked on harnessing the potential of his own unconscious by developing dreams, automatic writing, free association, and other procedures with the aim of liberating himself from the power of the conscious mind and all that was rational. *The Dream* was painted when Dali and his wife Gala Eluard were living uncomfortably at a fisherman's hut in Port Lligat. Dali's claustrophobic dream world today looks highly familiar and almost natural. This might be because it belongs to a universal unconscious or because his images have been so universally absorbed. In *Sleep* (1937), Dali recreated the soft and large head and nonexistent body that featured so often in his paintings. Both *Sleep* and *The Dream* have been of great interest to psychoanalysts. Dali's personification of sleep appears to be troubled and an extraordinary number of crutches are needed to support the head. Crutches are a trademark of Dali's work and seem to hint at the fragility of life. Nothing seems inherently stable and even the dog in this painting needs crutches to prop himself up.

LEFT: *The poet and artist William Blake, whose work includes* **Songs of Innocence and Experience (Plate 6** *is pictured here) claimed that the process of copper engraving, the method used for this particular piece, came to him in a dream he had involving his dead brother after he had spent hours trying to find a cheaper method of engraving.*

LEFT: *The Swiss psychologist Carl Jung was born in 1875. His theories, along with those of his contemporary, Sigmund Freud, lie at the root of all modern dream analysis.*

Jung and spirituality

Carl Gustav Jung (1875–1961) was one of the first Western thinkers to develop the concept of dream interpretation and to focus on the ability of dreams to enhance and enact a spiritual quest. He believed that dreams had the power to connect us to a collective unconscious (see page 12). Jung talked of level 3 or grand dreams which occur at the deepest level and have the power to communicate profound messages about our spiritual needs or directions. Jung named one of these archetypes Spirit, the opposite of matter. In such dreams the Spirit archetype may appear in the embodiment of someone who has died, a ghost, or more abstractly as an impression of infinity such as the sky or the sea. The wise old man or woman (see page 41) may also appear in spiritual dreams as a guide toward spirituality and the teacher of truths. These creative spiritual dreams can enable us to reclaim some of the deepest levels of potentiality that lie beneath the surface of our lives and relationships—even if we are baffled by the dream's sense of meaning and wonder.

The dream is an involuntary land of poetry.

JEAN PAUL RICHTER

Using your dreams to create

LUCID

Lucid dreaming is the term used to describe that state when we become aware that we are in the middle of a dream but this does not cause us to wake up from it. In these dreams we can learn to allow our consciousness to enter the dream state and take control of our dreams.

The label lucid dreaming was coined in 1913 by the Dutch physician William Van Eden. The process itself was actually well-known and had been documented long before Van Eden labeled it on behalf of Western science. Techniques to encourage dream control have been practiced in the East and in South American cultures for centuries. Tibetan Buddhists, for example, have always believed that the very purpose of the dream is to give the conscious mind an opportunity to control the unconscious mind.

At an advanced level lucid dreams can be used to answer questions about our desires and deepest emotions. For example, you might consciously create the symbol of a door in the dream. You might be able to control your dream scenario so that you open the door and behind it find the answer to a question. Another method is to create a wise counsellor whom you can consult in the dream. With lucid dreams comes the ability to question and formulate answers within a dream context.

False awakening occurs when we dream of waking up. It can feel rather odd because the dreamer is aware that they are dreaming but is unaware that the sensation of awakening is actually illusory too.

It is thought that people with a high degree of mental discipline are more likely to have lucid dreams. Therefore the best way to encourage lucid dreaming is to harness and encourage your mental strength. You can achieve this by paying close attention to the detail of your thought processes. This can be aided by giving a running commentary on your actions. Imagine stepping outside of your own head and observing all that you are feeling or thinking. Techniques such as meditation and visualization (exercises to help you with these are included in this book) can sharpen the thinking mind and facilitate lucid dreaming.

Study a significant object very closely just before you go to sleep. Notice how it is made, what it is made of. How did it come to be in your possession? Who is connected to this object and what are they like? What kinds of emotions are associated with the object? What kinds of stories are connected with the object? The shamans use this approach.

Visualize as often as you can during the day a simple daily action such as walking through the park, making a cup of tea, sitting in a train. If you then see this action in your dream it will make you conscious that you are dreaming and you may be able to tap into this and develop a lucid dream.

Auto-suggestion is another simple technique that might help you develop lucid dreams. At different times throughout the day tell yourself that when you go to sleep tonight you will become aware that you are dreaming. Tell yourself that you will be able to go into your dreams and affect them. Tell yourself that you know this will be able to happen and the more you think about it the more likely it will be to occur.

Take your time. Though belief that you can do it is an all-powerful tool, it is important not to rush this technique and to be patient. As with all new skills, it will take practice and this practice will need to be committed and ongoing if it is to have any impact on your abilities to develop lucid dreaming.

If after all this you fail to manage a lucid dream, then ask yourself to identify all the aspects of your dream that were wholly unlike real life and ask yourself why you were not able to recognize these as unreal, and this might give you some clues.

MEDITATION

Meditation is a powerful and useful tool for improving your concentration, thus allowing you to be more alert and aware of what is going on in your own mind during sleep. It can also improve your own access to your unconscious. If you can find the time and space to meditate last thing at night, it can really develop your powers of creativity—especially in relation to your dream world.

To begin with, if you have never tried this, just five minutes of meditation will do. Gradually as you become more accomplished this can be built up over time. The aim in meditation is to keep your mind alert and aware, yet relaxed at the same time. Your mind should be focused on individual stimuli rather than the busy flow of thoughts that usually preoccupy us.

- Notice the rise and fall of your breath. Count each breath silently from one to ten.

- As thoughts enter your head don't push them away, just let them be. Let them enter and leave your mind while you still concentrate on your breathing. It may take time, but as you focus on your breath the thought intrusions should happen less often.

- Shut your eyes or focus on a candle or on the third eye. This lies just above and between the eyes and is the focus of yoga philosophy.

- As you practice meditation regularly—at least on a daily basis—your concentration will improve and your consciousness will flow more easily.

- When you finish your meditation, keep this calm tranquil state in mind. Try to go straight to bed and keep your physical movements calm and unhurried so that they are in harmony with your state of mind.

- When you settle off to sleep allow your calm awareness to follow you.

The art of meditation is a complex one and much has been written on the subject. This simple exercise may give you a taster of how to use it to develop your own creative dream potential.

Problem solving in dreams

DESCARTES' DREAMS

In 1619 Descartes—one of the founders of modern philosophical and scientific thinking—was said to have had a series of three dreams in one night that radically changed his whole philosophy and course of thinking. At that time he was just twenty-three years old and already a gifted mathematician. He was turning to philosophy to develop his theories further. In the three dreams were a whirlwind, a clap of thunder, a dictionary and a book of poems. Descartes was a devout Christian and believed that the dreams were a message from God. He understood the whirlwind to be the drive to push his work forward. The clap of thunder represented a sign that he had hit on the truth in some way, and the two books revealed to him that poetry as well as philosophy had an important role to play in his work. Around the time of these dreams Descartes developed what he believed to be the greatest contribution to science at that time—the unity of the human sciences.

It may seem strange to think that dreams can help us with our problems, but from the many reports of scientists such as Descartes, this does seem to be a valid and common occurrence. The Russian chemist Mendeleyev had a dream in which he saw the whole periodic table, which tabulates the elements according their weights. The main techniques for opening up to problem solving in our dreams have long been recognized in other parts of the world, but until recently have been undervalued by Western psychology.

LAB DREAM CONTROL

Scientists and experimental psychologists have tried to develop machines to assist in the process of dream control. Such machines can be strapped to the dreamer's wrist, detect REM sleep (when rapid eye movement occurs), and then give out small electric shocks. These shocks are not meant to wake the dreamer, but just to raise their awareness and alert them to the fact that they are dreaming and therefore allow them to utilize their dreams through connecting their conscious to the unconscious. These gadgets are not practical for use outside the lab situation, but the techniques that are outlined here have the same desired affect, are much more practicable, and have been used for centuries across the world.

FREE ASSOCIATION

The method of free association was first developed and refined by Freud when he asked his patients to say whatever came into their minds to help get an insight into their unconscious. The basic rule that Freud employed was that the patient should report

Problem solving strategy

If you have a problem, allow your mind to work at finding a solution for a period of time. Don't be too intense and when you feel you have had enough, try to put the problem out of your mind and leave it to one side with the knowledge that the solution will come somehow at some time. Each time the problem enters your head tell yourself that there is no need to bother with it now because it will appear to you in your dreams. At bedtime as you drift off to sleep try to hold the problem in your mind. On waking try to write down the detail of any dream that you have had, even if at first glance it appears to have no relevance to the problem at hand. Don't study the dream at this stage, just note it down. Once you have identified all the dream images, try to free associate around the ones that strike you. Return to this exercise throughout the day and if the solution doesn't come immediately remember to be patient. Don't give up, and try each night. If you don't have a particular problem or dilemma you could find a mathematical problem or conundrum to test the theory and see if it works.

all their thoughts without reservation and that he or she should make no attempts to concentrate while doing so.

Free association works on the assumption that all lines of thought, whatever they are, tend to lead on to what is significant and that resistance is minimized by relaxation and maximized by concentration. The loose principles of free association can be used to facilitate creative thinking and help us to understanding our dreams. In order to do this you can take one significant aspect or person that emerges from your dream and then think around this. Play with it in your mind, turn it around, and study it from every angle. Try not to dissect it, just study it as it is. Notice what comes into your mind—a picture, word, or image. What comes next? Another image or idea? See what it suggests. If you get stuck you may think of this as a defense mechanism that is preventing you from getting too deep when you are not ready for it. You then might want to try again later or abandon the exercise. Only you can decide on the best course of action for your needs.

AMPLIFICATION

Although free association is a good technique for helping us to discover more about ourselves, it may take us away from the meaning of our dreams and the messages that are being conveyed. Jung utilized a process called amplification to facilitate an understanding of dream meanings. Jung's approach attaches more weight to dreams, and suggests that a dream is not really a disguise but means what it says. Jung's method is a way of elaborating on the dream.

ABOVE: *Descartes, one of the founders of modern philosophy pictured here in a portrait by Frans Hals, is said to have radically changed his course of thinking after a series of three dreams, which he believed were sent to him as a message from God.*

The best way to go about amplification is to select your important dream image and look at it from every angle. Don't think of a series of associations that take you away from the dream, but keep coming back to the image. Build up a group of associations around it rather than away from it.

No one method of dream interpretation is perfect. Free association can lead us astray from the image so that we lose the message, but amplification can get us stuck in the dream image with no wider considerations. It is probably worth utilizing both techniques at different times to best uncover the dream meanings for you own personal psyche and creativity.

CHAPTER 2

Family

If you cannot get rid of the family skeleton,
you may as well make it dance.

SIX WEEKS AFTER HIS DEATH MY FATHER APPEARED TO ME IN A DREAM. SUDDENLY HE STOOD

BEFORE ME AND SAID THAT HE WAS COMING BACK FROM HIS HOLIDAY. HE HAD MADE A GOOD

RECOVERY AND WAS NOW COMING HOME. I THOUGHT HE WOULD BE ANNOYED WITH ME FOR

HAVING MOVED INTO HIS ROOM, BUT NOT A BIT OF IT! NEVERTHELESS, I FELT ASHAMED BECAUSE

I HAD IMAGINED HE WAS DEAD. TWO DAYS LATER THE DREAM WAS REPEATED. MY FATHER HAD

RECOVERED AND WAS COMING HOME, AND AGAIN I REPROACHED MYSELF BECAUSE I HAD THOUGHT

HE WAS DEAD. LATER I KEPT ASKING MYSELF: 'WHAT DOES IT MEAN THAT MY FATHER RETURNS IN

DREAMS AND THAT HE SEEMS SO REAL?' IT WAS AN UNFORGETTABLE EXPERIENCE, AND IT FORCED

ME FOR THE FIRST TIME TO THINK ABOUT LIFE AFTER DEATH.

C.G. JUNG, *Memories, Dreams, Reflections,* **1963**

Dreams of family members, even if they are no longer living, can be imbued with reassuring messages. Such dreams may give us confidence or guidance when we feel stuck. In Jung's dream about his deceased father he started to question his ideas about the afterlife and how the living are contacted. For other analysts such a dream may describe Jung's current state of unconscious denial and they would suggest that at some level he may not have fully accepted his father's death.

Family dreams are particularly potent for us because our families are so deeply ingrained in our psyche. The way we were brought up and our family constellation have such profound effects on our psychological functioning that any dream of family members will probably have a unique and highly specific meaning to each dreamer, depending on their own experience and their related attitudes. Early family history, cultural or religious upbringing, sociocultural status, and sibling relations will all influence our family dreams.

PREVIOUS PAGE: *This Wilhelm Haller painting from the time of the Third Reich shows a 'perfect' young Aryan couple nurturing and educating their five children. Not surprisingly, it ignores any sense of diversity or difference in terms of a family unit, but this very traditional image with its austere parental figures may evoke some of the archetypal images that visit us in our dreams.*
RIGHT: *Early family history, our cultural and religious upbringing, our sibling relations and our relationship with our parents will all influence our dreams. Here Henry Moore parodies a typical family unit of a mother and father with their two children.*

The nature of the family is constantly evolving and in some respects the notion of the family is a socially constructed one.

What is a family?

The make-up of families is so different in different cultures and in different times that what we call family today, may not have been considered a family in earlier times and distant lands. The nature of the family is constantly evolving and in some respects the notion of the family is a socially constructed one. The theories that center on family relationships and their relationship to our dream worlds are culture-specific and should really be considered in that light.

In the most rigid sense, family refers to the fundamental kinship unit. In its smallest form it is thought to consist of mother, father, and offspring. In broader usage, though, the word family often refers to the extended family—grandparents, cousins, adopted children, aunts, and uncles, all operating as one social unit. Anthropologists and sociologists have many definitions of family based on their studies of different cultures in different parts of the world. By extension, the term family can be applied to any collection of closely or for-

mally related items or events. In maths, for example, we can refer to a family of curves. In psychology, we talk about a family of personality traits or attitudes. In biology, a family refers to a means of classification of related organisms that are grouped into some kind of order. In relation to our dreams, these ideas can be useful in helping us to understand what the idea of family means to us as individuals. Western concepts, such as sibling rivalry or the Oedipus complex, would make no sense if applied to those cultures where an uncle or a grandparent are no less significant than mothers or fathers. Understanding this may help us to think more broadly in interpreting our dreams with a family theme.

Families, dreams, and gender

Some studies claim that women tend to have more peaceful dreams than men. Gender itself may not be the significant variable here—rather it is family background that forms the all-important foundation for our dreams. Loving families are thought to sow the seed for a warm dream life. Disturbed family life has the opposite effect. It is surprising to note, however, that our brightest and most optimistic dreams often occur at times of sadness in our waking worlds. It is as if peaceful dreams are there to inspire us through these bad times. So, if you currently find yourself in a difficult family situation, your dream world may actually be quite bright and vivid.

Dreams about your mother may operate on a surface or a latent level, but they often tell you something about this most important of relationships. The mother attachment may be overpowering you right now and your dream may be urging you to break free. Inner independence from your mother is the first step to realizing your true self. On another level, mother dreams may symbolize the unconscious side of life and can be a source for growth. Mothers in dreams can represent the ultimate in authority figures. If your mother was authoritarian in life and often appears in your dreams it may be telling of your lack of confidence.

In the following two dreams both patients tell of a similar dream, namely the death of the mother. In one case a young woman went to Freud with a dream that she had when she was about four years old. In the dream she saw a lynx walking on the roof of her house. Then she saw something falling down and finally she saw her mother being carried dead out of the house. In his analysis, Freud concluded that the dream symbolized the patient's repressed wish that she had as a child to see her mother dead. Now because of this repression she believed that all her relatives hated her. She had said in her therapy with Freud that she didn't want to see her relatives again because of this. In support of this interpretation, the young woman also recalled that when she was a child some girls used to call her lynx-eyed. Also, when she was three, a tile had fallen off the roof, hitting her mother and making her bleed profusely.

The other case involves Jung's patient, who was also a young woman. In the dream which she described she came home very late and found the house as quiet as death. She went into the living room where she saw her mother hanging from the chandelier, her body swinging to and fro in the wind from the open window. Jung concluded from his dream analysis that the mother in this dream represented the archetypal symbol of the unconscious. The dream therefore tells the dreamer of the danger that her unconscious life is in. It is destroying itself. Jung also correctly predicted that this dream warned of serious physical illness.

These two dream mother scenarios are not necessarily contradictory. Rather they tell of the importance of using the dreamer's context to get the most out of understanding one's dreams. In Freud's dream case the knowledge that the girl used to be called lynx-eyed and that a tile fell off the roof was enough to support the interpretation that this dream did relate to the young woman's actual mother and thus indicated her repressed feelings towards her. In Jung's dream case there was no evidence of this kind, so a more abstract meaning was sought. (These dream interpretations, however, have been simplified for the purposes of this book.) The vital importance of studying each dream in context, with knowledge of the person's background, cannot be overemphasized.

Parent-child relations have been studied and written about since time began—from Joseph, the favored son, Cain and Abel, to mythological stepmothers and even Mrs. Robinson in the classic film *The Graduate*. Whole schools of family therapy have been developed to help address the issues that emerge within a family context, so no wonder that these figures are so powerful in our dream worlds.

Mother and mana

Jung believed that to achieve self-realization, individuation, or full happiness, one needs to explore one's unconscious and this can be done through our dreams. He described four stages which we need to pass through in order to do this. Stage one is the shadow; stage two is anima and animus; stage three is mana personalities, and stage four is the self. The other stages are referred to elsewhere in the book, but stage three has particular significance in terms of thought surrounding dreams of the mother.

Jung proposed that stage three is the second liberation from mother. The first liberation from mother occurs at stage two—when the anima or animus is integrated into conscious life. The second and richer liberation (i.e. stage three) is said to occur when one achieves a true sense of one's own identity and individuality. Stage three is said to occur when a man meets the Wise Old Man and a woman meets the Great Mother. Jung calls these archetypal images of wisdom and strength mana personalities. He chose this term because in non-Western communities anyone with extraordinary wisdom or power was said to filled with mana, a Melanesian word meaning holiness or the divine.

Jung warned that it is dangerous to be possessed by mana and that it can lead to megalomania. This might happen in the case of a woman who allows herself to become possessed by the Great Mother, leading her to believe that she has the power to save or protect the whole world. A man who becomes possessed by the Wise Old Man could falsely believe that he can accomplish anything. We may also project this mana onto another, and put our faith in great leaders or superheroes rather than own the power within ourselves. Jung suggested that the best way to manage mana was to allow it to be integrated into our personalities and our consciousness. It is most helpful to neither project it onto others nor repress it. In this way the wisdom within our unconscious is integrated within our conscious and we are balanced.

Common images of the Wise Old Man include magicians, prophets, kings, guides, doctors, priests, old men, gurus, and grandfathers. Common symbols of the Great Mother include goddesses or female figures to do with fertility, having large breasts and prominent vagina and buttocks.

Mana visualization

Try to visualize someone of the same sex who you believe is wise. See a picture of this man or woman in your mind's eye. What do you see? Now try to imagine that you are inhabiting that person's body. You take on their thoughts and feelings. Now ask yourself some questions from the point of view of this person. What are your priorities in life? What things do you value? What will you be doing in ten years' time? How do you see your life panning out? If you could give one piece of advice to young people, what would it be?

LEFT: **Dreams of the mother are thought to connect to the mana stage of our personality development, meaning wisdom and strength. It is thought that overdevelopment of this stage can lead to megalomania and dreams containing symbols of goddesses or female fertility figures, such as this statue of the Venus of Willendorf, may forewarn of this. This statuette is the most famous early image of a human, dating back to 24,000-22,000 BCE.**

Children

However old we are, we still continue to be someone's child, even if we also become someone's parent. The task of adolescence—of this miraculous and complex transformation from child to adult—is long and formidable. One is required to leave home, support oneself in the world, attract and possibly keep a sexual partner, and perhaps start a family of one's own. The bond to one's parents needs to be loosened, a job needs to be found and held, and one needs enough self-confidence and a well-enough developed persona to hold one's head up high in the world.

Dreams of children, whether it is yourself as a child or other children, are often highly significant and can have many meanings in your waking life. The child within a dream may be a symbol of your inner self. It may be a sign of your true potential—of the things of which you are truly capable. The child is untarnished by adult life and responsibility. It is unspoilt and is true in its nature. A dream of a child may tell of your own yearning or need to find that unspoilt part of yourself.

Many analysts suggest that child dreams tell of your need to be nurtured in some way. Dreams of undernourished or neglected children may often really be telling of the neglected part of yourself that lies within. Many theorists believe that within all of us lies a childhood part of ourselves that we never leave behind even though we may hide ourselves within adult bodies and lifestyles. At times the child within us will need care and attention and will need to be relieved from fear or guilt. At other times the child will need to be guided and corrected if it is to really grow up.

Others say that child dreams can tell of new beginnings, a new development in your psyche, a new philosophy or set of values. Dreams of children can imply a resolution or new phase within your psyche. The child within can represent a growth point or new phase of learning. If the child in your dream has a new aura it may represent the transcendent nature of the self. It is more than the conscious aspects of yourself. It holds together the opposites within, such as head and heart, creativity and rationality, masculinity and femininity.

SEPARATION AND SUFFOCATION

Dreams of suffocation can often tell of the dreamer's feelings toward separation and attachment and as such relate to experiences of childhood and dreams of children. These dreams often occur at times of change, for example when leaving home, or at times of illness or death. Dreams of suffocation can often tell of fears of being overwhelmed, dominated, or drowned by a powerful other. This person is likely to be a family figure.

Two highly influential psychoanalysts— John Bowlby and Donald Winnicott—wrote much about the concepts of separation and attachment. They suggested that a large

The child within a dream may be a symbol of your inner self. It may be a sign of your true potential...your own yearning or need to find that unspoilt part of yourself.

proportion of mental health functioning or mental health problems are associated with separation between infant and mother in childhood. Their suggestion is that separation in infancy not only causes distress for the baby at the time, but can also lead to difficulties in later life. Explanations of how this happens differ in their levels of complexity. In short, it is proposed that premature separation can lead to feelings of insecurity, which can increase feelings of hostility and ambivalence and can interfere with processes (such as introjection and identification) that affect ego development. This is said to trigger mourning at an age when the child is too young to manage these feelings and it can leave the child stuck in a state of despair or depression.

This theory is a rarity in the field of psychoanalysis insofar as it can be supported by scientific measurements or statistics, since separation between carer and infant are discernible facts that may occur as a consequence of death, hospitalization or desertion. The concept of separation, however, is not as straightforward as it initially seems, since only gross separation can be distinguished from maternal separation and it involves other factors like the age of the

child at the time of separation and the length of time of the separation. Dreams of separation, loss, and abandonment may be informative for the dreamer, as they may tell of an unresolved separation where feelings of mourning and ambivalence toward the parent or other family figure have not been fully explored and dealt with.

It seems that Jung himself went through a difficult separation with his own mother, which had repercussions on his social functioning. Jung's mother was said to have experienced a depressive illness in his early childhood which resulted in a prolonged period of separation from Jung when he was just three years old—the time of this, his first dream. The dream reveals much about his family, his culture, and his life. For the sake of this chapter, our focus will be on its meaning in relation to his mother and his attachment to her.

In the dream I was in this meadow. Suddenly I discovered a dark, rectangular, stone-lined hole in the ground. I had never seen it before. I ran forward curiously and peered down into it. Then I saw a stone stairway leading down. Hesitantly and fearfully I descended. At the bottom was a doorway with a round arch, closed off by a green curtain. It was a big, heavy curtain of worked stuff like brocade, and it looked very sumptuous. Curious to see what might be hidden behind, I pushed it aside. I saw before me in the dim light a rectangular chamber about thirty feet long. The ceiling was arched and of hewn stone. The floor was laid with flagstones, and in the centre a red carpet ran from the entrance to a low platform. On this platform stood a wonderfully rich golden

throne. I am not certain, but perhaps a red cushion lay on the seat. It was a magnificent throne, a real king's throne in a fairy tale. Something was standing on it which I though at first was a tree trunk twelve to fifteen feet high and about one and a half to two feet thick. It was a huge thing, reaching almost to the ceiling. But it was of curious composition: it was made of skin and naked flesh, and on the top there was something like a rounded head with no face and no hair. On the very top of the head was a single eye, gazing motionlessly upwards.

It was fairly light in the room, although there were no windows and no apparent source of light. Above the head, however, was an aura of brightness. The thing did not move, yet I had the feeling that it might at any moment crawl off the throne like a worm and creep towards me. At that moment I heard from outside and above me my mother's voice. She called out, 'Yes, just look at him. That is the man-eater!' That intensified my terror even more, and I awoke sweating and scared to death. For many nights afterward I was afraid to go to sleep, because I feared I might have another dream like that.

Jung's mother spent several months in a hospital in Basel, and presumably her illness had something to do with the difficulty in the marriage which Jung described at different times. In her absence Jung was cared for by an aunt, but was troubled by this separation and developed a type of nervous eczema. "From then on I always felt mistrustful when the word 'love' was spoken. The feeling I associated with 'woman' was for a long time that of innate unreliability. 'Father' on the other hand meant reliability and powerlessness." Emilie Jung's emotional withdrawal into a state of depression may be symbolized the lack of maternal protectiveness in the dream.

SEPARATION ANXIETY

Anxiety is thought to occur at the prospect of being separated from someone who is considered to be essential for your survival. More often than not, separation anxiety occurs in relation to another family member or spouse, as these are normally the people with whom we maintain the closest relationships. Separation anxiety may be quite objective—for example where it occurs in infancy when the parent figure is absolutely essential for the survival of the child. It can also be a neurotic occurrence, however, where the presence of another person is used as a defense against some other form of anxiety. In both cases two factors are involved: dread of some unspecified danger, either from the outside or from mounting internal tension, and dread of losing the object believed capable of protecting. Dreams can provide helpful clues that can facilitate the management of such feelings.

DIVINE CHILD

The divine child is thought to be an embodiment of innocence and purity. In the dream scenario the divine child usually appears as an infant or new baby who is very vulnerable but also powerful. This infant is able to generate action and transform imagery. This archetypal image is thought to remind us of our origins and of a time when we were free from the oppressive powers of the ego—by which we mean the conscious aspect of the self. The appearance of the divine child in our dreams can reawaken this early untapped potential and help to reduce the struggle of adulthood.

You can reconnect with the child within yourself if you try to imagine what you as a baby might feel and experience in the world. You can help this process by observing a newborn baby or you can try to imagine it in your mind's eye. Try to visualize a time when the whole world was new and fresh and everything was there to be discovered. Imagine how the world must have looked, felt, sounded, and smelled. Notice how infants put objects in their mouth to try to fully understand their shape, texture, and form. Can you recall just how exciting (and overwhelming) it was when everything was so new?

Carly is nine-year-old girl who has persistent nightmares, in which she dreams that she goes to school in the morning but by the afternoon no one comes to collect her. In fact Carly and her mother are being seen by a psychologist at their local health center because Carly is refusing to go to school and spends many days at home with her mother. She fears going to school and it seems that she fears being parted from her mother. During discussion it appears that when Carly is not at school she and her mother do everything together. They visit relatives, they visit the shops, they play together. Carly's mother seems to enjoy having Carly around. The problem started six months ago when her mother split up from Carly's dad. It seems, then, that Carly's nightmares and waking experiences of separation anxiety do not arise solely from Carly's own internal state, but rather that anxiety may be increased because of the vulnerability of Carly's mother—who may be also feeling unprotected and lonely.

Dreams of an older sibling may represent parts of your self or ego that are currently neglected.

Brother and sister

The appearance of our siblings in our dreams may be a direct representation of them, or they may actually stand for someone else in our lives. Some analysts suggest that all dream characters represent aspects of ourselves anyway. So when interpreting dreams of siblings, it is worth bearing in mind these three levels of meaning. In childhood and later on in life, a sibling is often the object of jealousy and envy. For a firstborn, feelings of jealousy and rage can emerge as the child might feel displaced by their younger sibling and might crave the level of attention that they once had from their mother or carer. Often we can carry these hostile feelings with us throughout life, but the resentments may take adult form—for example they may be linked to money or caring for one's parents in older age and who does what. If you feel that you are involved with sibling grievances and that these also appear in your dreams in various forms, it is worth addressing these issues and acknowledging what they are really about, because they may date back to early childhood events that were in fact beyond your control.

Dreams of an older sibling may represent parts of your self or ego that are currently neglected. This is what Jung called the shadow (discussed in more detail in Chapter 3 on Fear and Chapter 10 on Change). People often project their shadow onto siblings of the same sex, and if it is not projected it may express itself in all kinds of ways—such as rudeness or other antisocial behavior. When dreams of the opposite sexed sibling occur, this may be some expression of your anima or animus. It could also represent the tension or union of opposites in some way. The unconscious and conscious elements of the psyche could be combining to create harmony and balance—if you let them.

CHAPTER 3

Fear

I don't use drugs, my dreams are frightening enough.

M.C. ESCHER

FEAR IS A COMMONLY EXPERIENCED DREAM EMOTION. A DREAM THAT CONTAINS A LARGE ELEMENT OF FEAR IS USUALLY KNOWN AS A NIGHTMARE. A NIGHTMARE WILL NEARLY ALWAYS REPRESENT SOMETHING WITHIN YOUR UNCONSCIOUS MIND. ERNEST JONES MAINTAINED THAT NIGHTMARES WERE ALWAYS AN EXPRESSION OF CONFLICT BETWEEN UNCONSCIOUS SEXUAL DESIRE AND FEAR. OTHER DREAM EXPERTS BELIEVE THAT NIGHTMARES SERVE TO PUNISH THE DREAMER FOR SOME SIN AGAINST THEIR OWN CONSCIENCE.

Art and literature have strongly focused on the notion of dream fear. A classic example is Edvard Munch's haunting painting *The Scream*, which vividly depicts the intense feelings of anxiety that can be experienced in a dream or waking state. The symbolic dream fear can return to haunt us in waking life, so that as with *The Scream,* dream and reality become confused.

Common dream symbols connected with fear are blackness, fire, hell, demons, and devils. Dostoevsky in *The Brothers Karamazov* (1888) wrote "I sometimes dream of devils. It's night, I'm in my room, and suddenly there are devils everywhere. In all the corners and under the table, and they open doors, and behind the doors there are crowds of them..." Where the feared object in a dream seems evil, it may well represent some part of one's inner self that is trying to destroy the successful or calm aspect of self. Demons and devils are said to represent part of the mind that has been repressed. That aspect, therefore, should be treated tenderly in order to take on those demons so that they do not attack the positive aspects of the dreamer's world.

In ancient times demonic possession was probably the term used for what we now describe as the conscious ego being taken over by unconscious forces—fear and anger for example. The Judeo-Christian and Islamic traditions described the Devil as a horned fertility god. Devil dreams, with their links to Satan and fertility, may indicate a new phase in life, new beginnings, and fertilization rather than negative events.

A father figure who appears in a frightening dream is likely to express notions of guilt. Self-depreciation often stems from childhood fears of a father's perceived or sometimes real disapproval. Freud's controversial theory of castration anxiety proposed that all fears of punishment were triggered by the fear of castration. In males this is connected with what Freud termed the Oedipus complex (see page 128), which is said to occur when a boy desires his mother and consequently has feelings of envy toward his father, and fears that his father may punish him for having these feelings.

Many analysts propose that a fear of the mother may be represented in dreams through symbols of spiders, water, dragons, and crocodiles.

Some say that the task of human life is to convert the negative devilish energy within ourselves into positively charged energy, which creates life-enhancing powers. Confronting the devils and anxieties within our dream lives, as many have done through the use of the arts, can facilitate the journey toward positive emotional well-being.

PREVIOUS PAGE: *This 15th century Italian painting entitled* **The Last Judgement: The Pain of Hell,** *depicts a vision of hell including demons and the devil—common dream symbols connected with fear.*
RIGHT: *This painting portrays an Italian farmer who awakes after sleeping to find his room full of demons —a frightening dream symbol which represents part of the inner self that is trying to destroy the successful or calmer aspect of self. Other common dream symbols connected with fear include blackness, fire and hell.*

Nightmares

Historically nightmares were thought to happen when the dreamer was visited at night by demons. The mare was thought to be a monstrous being that descended upon sleeping souls to satisfy its lust. The Freudian view of the nightmare is that it contains repressed sexual desires. A more widely accepted view is that these bad dreams force us to confront actions or emotions that we feel particularly strongly about in our waking life. Nightmares allow us to express our deepest fears and fantasies which, due to the social constraints of everyday life, are rarely explored. As the nightmare unfolds, the pulse and respiratory rate of the dreamer can double. The dreamer usually escapes into consciousness on the cusp of the nightmare, but images often remain in the mind's eye and return to stalk us on a regular basis. Some people become so troubled by their bad dreams that they are afraid to go to sleep and remain in a state of semi-slumber or hypnogogia.

POST TRAUMATIC STRESS AND THE NIGHTMARE

Nightmares can occur as part of the psychological disorder now commonly termed post traumatic stress disorder or PTSD. This disorder occurs in response to some event—combat, natural disaster, sexual attack, airplane crash, for example—that would be traumatic for anyone. The symptoms of PTSD consist of reexperiencing this traumatic event—usually through dreams but also through waking flashbacks. The sufferer will usually avoid situations similar to the traumatic one and will generally have a heightened feeling of anxiety, guilt, and arousal. They may also experience "reduced responsiveness" or an emotional numbness.

The effects of PTSD on veterans from Vietnam have been well documented, particularly in relation to the horrific dreams they have had.

I can't get these memories out of my mind! The images come back in vivid detail, triggered by the most inconsequential things, like a door slamming or the smell of stir-fried pork. Last night I went to bed, was having a good sleep for a change. Then in the early morning a storm-front passed through and there was a bolt of crackling thunder. I awoke instantly, frozen in fear. I am right back in Vietnam, in the middle of the monsoon season at my guard post. I am sure I'll get hit in the next volley and convinced I will die. My hands are freezing, yet sweat pours from my entire body. I feel each hair on the back of my neck standing on end. I can't catch my breath and my heart is pounding. I smell a damp sulfur smell.
Davis 1992, in Ronald J. Comer, *Abnormal Psychology*, 1995.

Clinicians believe that dreams and other processing techniques can be used therapeutically to relieve symptoms in the longer term. In many cases a clinician (a psychiatrist or a psychologist) will help the sufferer visualize the traumatic scene in great detail and urge him or her to hold onto this image until the feelings of anxiety have passed—a technique known as flooding. After each of these flooding exercises, the practitioner would then switch to positive imagery and lead the client through some relaxation exercises. In response to this treatment flashbacks and nightmares can diminish.

INCUBUS ATTACKS

Nightmares are some of the most mysterious dreams and still are not fully understood. In these dreams a feeling of terror seems to overcome us for no apparent reason. Often this is accompanied by a feeling of being trapped or crushed. This crushing kind of nightmare is also known as an incubus attack. Some theorists claim that this dream is physically produced. They suggest that we experience this stifling sensation because we have had difficulties breathing in the dream. Although incubus attacks are quite rare,

ABOVE: *A common form of nightmare is when you feel as if you are unable to move or cry out. Here in Jean Bruller's painting, the dreamer's screams go unheard. There is a physical explanation for this sensation—these occur in the REM phase of sleep when the body is actually immobolized.*

they seem to occur most commonly with children. It is suggested that if a child wakes screaming from such a nightmare, you should comfort them and reassure them that everything is all right and that the dream will not happen again. In fact there will rarely be two incubus attacks on the same night and it may take weeks for there to be another, if at all. Although they are highly distressing, there is no evidence to show that incubus attacks cause any damage to the dreamer. If they recur in adults, it may be worth seeking some health advice.

a violent conflict between a certain unconscious sexual desire and an intense fear.

ERNEST JONES

'On the Nightmare' by Ernest Jones

One of the most prolific students of the nightmare was Ernest Jones, who wrote a book called *On the Nightmare*. Jones wrote that the nightmare is always the expression of "a violent conflict between a certain unconscious sexual desire and an intense fear." He suggested that healthy people never had nightmares and that in men their unconscious fears were linked to feelings about their own sexuality and homosexual inclinations. He said that most men would be disgusted to have such tendencies and would try to repress these urges. This would result in a conflict and lead to the experience of nightmare. Critics have found this explanation too simplistic. Other explanations of the nightmare are equally shallow. For example, Calvin Hall believes that nightmares occur in order to punish the dreamer against the sins of his conscience *(The Meaning of Dreams)*. In *The Dream Game* Anne Faraday supports this argument through her own experience. She says that she has frequent nightmares including "many nightmares that were almost certainly self punishment… these usually took the form of imprisonment or execution." Anne Faraday also draws on Jung's theory of the shadow, which suggests that the shadow or our dark side is represented by unconscious desires that we try to repress during our waking lives.

LEFT: *Henry Fuseli's* **The Nightmare** *portrays a common dream aspect. A widely accepted view is that the nightmare is a way of forcing us to confront fears, anxieties, and emotions that we feel strongly about in waking life. Fuseli's painting shows a woman in the grips of a demonic nightmare, and clearly expresses the distress that she is suffering. A copy of this painting hung in Freud's apartment in Vienna in the 1920s.*

RIGHT: *Francisco Goya's painting depicting the execution of the defenders of Madrid during the Napoleonic invasion of Spain, illustrates two common fear sensations within dreams—that of being killed and the feeling of entrapment. A dream where you think you are about to be killed does not mean that you are about to die but instead shows that you are carrying the weight of an undesirable personality trait that you need to rid yourself of. Entrapment, meanwhile, suggests self-punishment, and the shadow of our darker side which we tend to repress during waking hours.*

The shadow

Jung's notion of the shadow—the hidden opposite aspects of our psyche that are not apparent within the persona—is quite useful in helping us to understand the meaning of our nightmares and fearful dreams. In Jungian analysis the dreamer is strongly encouraged to find out more about their shadow. They work to accept their shadow and even befriend him. We frequently recognize the characteristics of the shadow in personalities that we do not like or even despise. Because our greatest fears and prejudices are so deeply concealed, we are reluctant to recognize, let alone explore them. So we often project those characteristics onto other people, thereby abdicating responsibility for ourselves. Jung and others emphasize the fact that other characters in our dreams and nightmares often represent different aspects of ourselves. It takes a brave person to face their shadows and often this is best done in analysis of some kind. However, dreams and nightmares can be a useful starting point from which to begin this exploration.

Fearful dreams of attack are commonplace and can be linked to the Jungian archetypal concept of the shadow. Like every other complex, the shadow also has its archetypal core—the archetype of the enemy, the attacker, the evil intruder, the deadly stranger. This is thought to be part of adaptive and evolutionary survival equipment. As such, the archetype of the attacker is said to come to the fore in early infancy because in order to survive all animals need to be wary of anything strange and potentially hostile. As the animal or human grows older, the archetypal attacker nucleus develops into a more detailed picture of that which is threatening, and often reflects what the parent perceives as threatening.

The shadow in literature

Robert Louis Stevenson in The Strange Case of Dr. Jekyll and Mr. Hyde *tells an intriguing story which utilizes the notion of the shadow and unconscious projection. Dr. Jekyll is presented as an intellectual bachelor obsessed and intrigued by his own shadow. The difficulty is that Dr. Jekyll is completely unaware of this repressed aspect of his psyche, and rather than assimilating or integrating the darker aspects of himself into his consciousness, Dr. Jekyll becomes possessed by it as he transforms himself into the monstrous Mr. Hyde.*

The Faust legend provides another good example of the coexistence of these two different aspects of the personality within one person. Faust's obsessional pursuit of knowledge results in an unbalanced intellectual development. He suppresses other aspects of his self-potential and becomes disillusioned with life. However, as in most cases the suppressed aspect of the self needs attention because it has not vanished, it is merely hidden within. In Faust's case it becomes a shadow-intruder, the Devil figure Mephistopheles. Faust projects onto Mephistopheles all the power and strength that has been suppressed within himself. If Faust had been aware of Jungian thinking, he may have owned this aspect of his psyche and become more balanced and whole.

Faust and Dr. Jekyll, unlike Oscar Wilde's Dorian Gray, at least try to address their dark shadows rather than merely presenting a perfectly untarnished persona to the outside world. Perhaps that is why generations of literature lovers have been fascinated by these stories. These characters dare to take on the challenge of the shadow.

The paralysis nightmare

A common and frightening form of nightmare is to dream that we are paralyzed—unable to move. Dreams of paralysis almost always occur in the phase of REM (rapid eye movement) sleep when we are actually physically immobilized. Therefore this suggests that there are some physical explanations for the paralysis nightmare. It is generally known that someone who tosses and turns in the midst of a night's sleep is unlikely to be having a nightmare. Part of the fear that lies within a nightmare is the fear that we are unable to move, or cry out for help, which usually mirrors some feeling of being stuck that we have in our waking life or our unconscious minds.

Jenny's dream

Jenny dreamt that she was on holiday with her husband, his sister, and her family and his parents. In fact, that summer she and her husband had planned to go abroad with her in-laws and Jenny was not looking forward to it very much. She was concerned about not being able to do her own thing and feared being restricted by her husband's family. In the dream the whole family was lounging on the beach. The children were playing happily in the sand when suddenly Jenny felt her area of sand turn to quicksand and her feet got stuck and she was unable to move. As she remained paralyzed in her patch of quicksand, she was unable to do anything but witness her in-laws leaving the beach. They packed up all the belongings and took her husband and children. As they left, they all laughed conspiratorially at Jenny and left her to her fate as nighttime drew in. Jenny woke up in a cold sweat.

The monster nightmare

Generally you should try to face the monsters that appear in your nightmares. In this way you should be able to take control and overcome them in some way. Knowledge is power and when you finally manage to see and understand the monsters in your dreams then their potency will usually diminish. In fact when you look the monster in the eye, it may even become comical. Monsters generally are concrete representations of what we perceive to be burdens in our waking life and can be usefully worked with to empower ourselves and to create a more balanced inner world. Once you recognize your monster you may even be able to start a dialogue with it and work through the situation in some way.

Mark's dream
Mark dreamt that he was in the shower getting ready for work. As he was washing himself with the bar of soap, the soap magically transformed itself into a beautiful delicate jewel that then became an ugly, slippery alien-type of monster. It slithered out of Mark's hand and grew and grew in size as Mark tried to turn the shower off and escape from the bathroom. The soap transformed itself further and started to sprout millions of tentacles that wrapped themselves around Mark's limbs and torso until he could hardly breathe. Finally Mark woke up screaming. His girlfriend tried to comfort him. Mark thought about the possible meaning of the dream and connected it to the unconscious thoughts and feelings he was currently experiencing toward his girlfriend. This was quite a new relationship for Mark, who was unaccustomed to the nature of the commitment. Even though he was really serious about Helena, he feared this level of closeness. He had once had his trust abused in a previous relationship and was wary to trust again. The soap that became a beautiful creature and then a monster was Mark's demon that he needed to face. He feared the intensity of emotion that he had with Helena and felt that she might not be all that she seemed and might even abuse his trust once more. He used the dream to move himself forward and discuss some of these emotions with Helena. In a way he was relieved to do this and was pleased that his unconscious had alerted him to this level of concern.

Nightmare exercises

A useful way to gain control over nightmares is to visualize the nightmare image or monster just before you fall asleep and try to transform it in your mind's eye. Picture the dream image or monster as clearly as you can. Notice how it all looks, observe the color, try to hear the sounds, notice the smells, notice the looks on everyone's faces. Then with equal force and clarity imagine the dream monster tamed by the power of wisdom and knowledge. It can sometimes help to imagine knowledge in a humanized form, as a dream helper, a knight in shining armor or a dream warrior of some sort. In some scary dreams there is no clear enemy or monster, but things that seem good and natural can turn bad before your very eyes. The dream hero can be visualized as a guide to help us point out hidden dangers before they surprise us. Positive and creative visualisation can help to strip bad dreams of their terror and reduce their power over us.

Animal nightmares

Animals that appear in our dreams are usually said to represent different aspects of our selves or even the animal part of our nature. If you dream of an animal in a nightmare, take time to think about what this animal represents to you. Is it the aggressiveness that of a lion or a tiger, or is it the timidity of mouse? Perhaps this animal part of your nature is being repressed in some way, and the appearance of it in your nightmares is a scream to uncage and face the beast within you.

Ways to manage you nightmare animals

Some people find that after they have had a dream with a scary animal in it they write down all their waking associations with that creature. Notice what it means to you, your experience with it in the past, what happened in the dream with the animal, and how you could overcome any difficulties in the future. Other people like to draw the animal in their dreams. They observe the detail—the color of the eyes, the type of skin or fur, the way it carried itself. Both of theses exercises help to reduce the size of the animal to reasonable proportions and thus help you to deal with what was once an overwhelming fear.

Anxiety dreams

Jung said that a dream "shows inner truth or reality… as it really is: not as I conjecture it to be, and not [as the dreamer] would like it to be, but as it is." It is important therefore to stand up to your dream, however frightening it may be, and not shrink away from it. A fearful dream in which you encounter or become a killer can be horrifying and can stay with you for life. However, such a dream does not mean that you are going to be killed nor that you will kill anyone. It may mean, however, that you are carrying the weight of an undesirable personality characteristic that needs to be extinguished. Like all other dreams, anxiety dreams require some knowl-

edge of context and feeling before any reasonable interpretation can be made of them. Generally the meaning of an anxiety dream does not necessarily depend on the content of the dream. In order to fully understand its meaning, Freud suggested that the analyst needs some understanding of the determinants of the neurotic anxiety. Anxiety is one of the ego's reactions to repressed wishes that may have become overly powerful.

Freud used the concept of anxiety to describe those fearful emotions that we experience in our dreams and in our waking lives. The main body of Freudian theory centers on how psychic defense mechanisms help us manage unconscious experiences of anxiety or fear. The ego can employ ego-defenses to reduce the tensions between the conflicting demands of the superego (society) and the instinct (id). An understanding of these defense mechanisms can be very fruitful for the full interpretation of one's dream images. Freud identified eleven defense mechanisms, all of which can appear in our dreams in different guises: repression, regression, rationalization, projection, compensation, sublimation, displacement, identification, reaction formation, symptoms, neuroses, and psychoses.

You can use all or any of these concepts to shed light on the meaning of dreams. Useful signifiers of repressed wishes include hostility toward parents, siblings or others.

The two chairs exercise

Fritz Perls, the leading Gestalt psychotherapist, used this method for much of his analysis, particularly in understanding the meaning of his patient's dreams. You can use this technique up to a point to facilitate your understanding of your own dreams. This technique is especially helpful for aiding the interpretation and working through your nightmares.

Take two chairs and place them opposite each other. Sit in one chair yourself but imagine that your nightmare character— whether it is an animal, a monster or some other shadowy figure—is in the chair opposite you. Ask the character why you are unable to understand it. Then move over to the other chair and really try to get into the role of that dream character and answer the question. Begin a dialogue between yourself and the dream monster as you move between chairs to take on each part. Let the process go on for some time until it draws to a natural end. Hopefully, eventually one of the characters—probably the feared dream character—will deliver an "aha!" that strikes a chord with you. When this happens the meaning or intent of the dream should be more clearly revealed.

CHAPTER 4

Conflict

When the fight begins with himself, / A man's worth something.

NEARLY EVERYONE LIVES WITH SOME DEGREE OF CONFLICT IN THEIR DAILY LIVES. THIS DOES NOT MEAN THAT WE ALL GO ABOUT OUR BUSINESS FEELING AGGRESSIVE OR HOSTILE, BUT CONFLICT IS THE BREAD AND BUTTER OF OUR CONSCIOUS AND UNCONSCIOUS LIVES. EVERY HUMAN BEING EXPERIENCES VARYING LEVELS OF ANXIETY, TENSION, FEAR, AND GUILT. IT THEREFORE MAKES SENSE TO USE ALL THE METHODS WE CAN TO TRY TO UNDERSTAND THESE CONFLICTS AND TO HELP US FEEL MORE AT EASE WITH OURSELVES AND THE WORLDS WITHIN WHICH WE MUST FUNCTION. OUR DREAMS CAN BE AN INVALUABLE TOOL TO FACILITATE THIS PROCESS. UNDERSTANDING THE MESSAGES OF OUR DREAMS CAN LEAD TO FULLER PSYCHIC KNOWLEDGE AND BETTER EMOTIONAL HEALTH. DREAMS CAN BE USED TO DEVELOP AN UNDERSTANDING OF CONFLICT THAT CAN THEN CREATE AN EXPERIENCE OF WHOLENESS OR PSYCHOLOGICAL HEALING.

Conflict in dreams

A dream: two groups of men were fighting each other. The group to which I belonged had captured one of our opponents, a gigantic naked man. Five of us clung to him, one to the head, two on either side by his arms and legs. Unfortunately we had no knife, no one had one. But since for some reason there was no time to lose and an oven stood near by whose extraordinarily large cast-iron door was red-hot, we dragged the man to it, held one of his feet close to the oven until the foot began to smoke, pulled it back again until it stopped smoking, then thrust it close to the door again. We monotonously kept this up until I awoke, not only in cold sweat but with my teeth actually chattering.
Franz Kafka, *Diaries,* April 20, 1916

Not all dreams of conflict are as violent or as disturbing in nature as this one by the Czech existentialist writer Franz Kafka. Sometimes conflict dreams may be connected to images of fighting, war, and aggression. More subtle conflict dreams, however, can be linked to images of abandonment,

loss of control or fear. Even the most self-assured people can experience pangs of insecurity at times, and this conflict between self-confidence and fear of the world can often emerge within a dream scenario. For example, dreams of missing a bus, train or airplane may tell of the tension in the dreamer about failing to achieve a certain expectation that he or she had. Similarly, dreams of earthquakes, landslides, and volcanoes point toward some notion of inner turmoil or emotional conflict as the very foundations of the dreamer's world are being disturbed. Dreams of anchors and lifeboats may also tell of a fight for survival— another representation of the struggle or conflict that each of us encounters in our quest through life.

John's dream

John dreams that he is at the theater watching his favorite play Pygmalion, by George Bernard Shaw. The story tells of an East London flower girl who is picked up by two academics, who, for a small wager, try to teach her how to become upper class. John dreams that the play is drawing to a climax and Eliza Doolittle, the protagonist, is about to leave the professor's household to embark on her journey. In the dream John gets onto the stage and shouts at the actors, begging them to stop. He explains to them that Eliza will never survive in the outside world and begs them to end the play there rather than continue to the end. On waking reflection, John makes his associations to the story and the dream and realizes just how much he identifies with the story of Pygmalion. He was brought up as the son of

a dockyard laborer in an inner city area. However, he has just secured a place to go to Cambridge University to do a science degree and is anxious about his ability to fit in. The conflict between his working-class background and the potentially upper-class career that lies ahead lives within him and is brought to the surface through this dream.

> ### Dream prompts
>
> *If you have a dream of conflict try to notice what it was that triggered the dream. How does this relate to your conscious life? If you are unable to find a connection, can you make any random associations to the dream? Was there an opponent in the dream? If there was an opponent, could this be a hidden part of yourself? Was your opponent serious or playful? Was anyone in the dream really hurt by the fight or was it resolved before it got too dangerous? Was hostility increased or reduced by the conflict? Was the conflict resolved and if so, how? Could you use the method of resolution again in your waking life or in a visualization task?*

PREVIOUS PAGE: *Conflict dreams often contain gruesome and explicit images of actual fighting or war, as in Henri Rousseau's piece,* **La Chevauchee de la Discorde.**

ABOVE: *Dreams of volcanos, such as Vesuvius, pictured here, point toward some notion of inner turmoil or conflict.*

The conflict of forbidden desires

Forbidden desires are often repressed in our unconscious because we may fear them. When this happens, a conflict often ensues between our unconscious drives, which want us to explore them, and our conscious mind, which wants to keep these desires repressed. Dream analysts suggest that we must allow ourselves to explore this conflict and allow forbidden desires a proper mode of expression in our waking lives. They say that by doing this our personality becomes more balanced. Our dreams can therefore be used to guide us on this journey.

Freud maintained that in our dreams our instincts and desires (id) try to communicate with the ego (the conscious part of ourselves). When we sleep our ego relaxes and lets the id come through. However, the superego is still on duty when we are asleep, operating at an unconscious level. If the id's desires are in conflict with the moral, social, and cultural values of our time, then the superego will intervene and censor the message that the id is sending. The consequence is that the message from our unconscious mind comes through in a distorted form. According to Freud most dreams are disguised messages.

To wish death upon someone close to us will inevitably bring with it conflicting feelings of guilt and shame and will probably be repressed. Sometimes they will become highly disguised, so instead of having a dream about killing our sister or brother we may have an anxiety dream in which we are worried about their health. The conflict between unconscious rage and conscious shame is then neatly disguised. Similarly, sexual desires are often repressed because they disgust the superego— hence the emergence of another psychic conflict.

Pregnant women are often said to have vivid dreams. This may be because the expectant mother is about to be involved in the biggest life change of all and there may be many conflicting emotions about the whole process of birth and raising a child, with all the implications that this brings. Farhanna was six months pregnant and had a recurrent dream in which she left her baby in the airing cupboard to shrivel up and die. On waking she was horrified at what she had done and feared her capabilities as a mother. When she wrote down this dream she realized that it told of her conflicting wish to keep her life as it was and not have it destroyed by this new and needy creature. At the same time it told of her anxieties about being able to cope with the responsibility of a new baby.

It is often forgotten that Freud himself had deeply divided feelings about his own father. He was highly affected by his father's death, and at the time he developed many symptoms that he himself defined as hysterical. The night before his father's funeral he dreamt of a placard showing the words *you are requested to shut the eyes*. On further exploration Freud wondered whether it actually read *you are requested to shut one eye*. Some might say that this is a conflict for interpretation in itself, and that a choice would need to be made before free association could be considered. Freud freely associated along both lines and came to the same conclusion. First, his father's eyes were closed in death, so it was connected to surface experiences. Freud also knew that there were things about his relationship with his father to which he would rather have shut his eyes, but which had been stirred up when he died. He also recalled the conflicting wishes of his father and his family about the style of the funeral. Freud saw that he had turned a blind eye to the wishes of his family for an elaborate funeral, bearing in mind those of his father for a simple one. The two sentences linked the latent content of the dream with surface preoccupations with the actual funeral.

RIGHT: *Achilles and his army are depicted fighting violently over the dead body of his closest friend, Patroclus, who was killed in war by Hector. While many conflict-related dreams may include images of fighting and war more subtle conflict dreams, however, may suggest feelings of abandonment, loss of control or fear in waking life.*

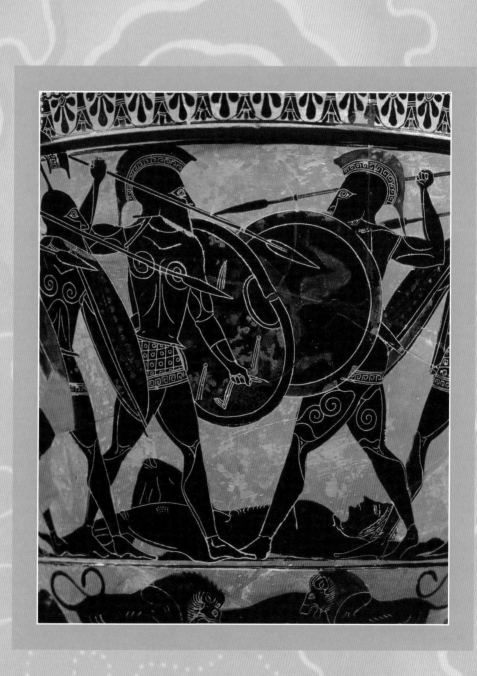

Jung argued that our conscience is the voice of inner wisdom that will lead us to ultimate selfhood.

Opposed forces of the psyche

What you ought to do, that is your conscience, is essentially socially constructed and consists of those ideas and beliefs that were imprinted onto you when you were growing up. These continue to be driven home through media, government, friends, and family. The conflict between the needs of the individual and the needs of society are as old as the world, and there are no easy answers to this on-going conflict. Inevitably, some degree of compromise must take place.

This is not to say that social norms are always right, however. You will need to think back to your own upbringing to determine whether your conscience is unusually harsh or severe, perhaps due to a restrictive or repressive upbringing by your parents. Whatever the case, the conflict needs to be addressed, which often means allowing the natural drives a little more expression in your waking life. This, obviously, does not mean going off to kill your mother, but rather exploring your negative feelings toward her. This can often be within the dream scene format.

Vicky's dream

Vicky was attending weekly individual psychotherapy with the aim of working through some childhood difficulties. One week she brought a dream to her therapist in which the therapist had gone to answer the door to Vicky but in the process had fallen down the stairs, twisted her ankle, and seriously damaged her back. In the dream Vicky looked through the letterbox and saw her therapist paralyzed, lying at the foot of the stairs unable to move. In their discussion Vicky linked this dream to her unconscious feelings of anger toward the therapist for not doing a good enough job in their work together. This was linked back to feelings that Vicky held about her own mother, who was represented by her therapist, and the way in which she cared for Vicky when she was a child.

WHAT WE ARE VERSUS WHAT WE COULD BE

Jung suggested that a conflict emerges between what we are and our full human potential of what we could be. Jung argued that our conscience (or superego) is the voice of inner wisdom that will lead us to ultimate selfhood. In this way it is conflict itself that keeps the conscience alive in the psyche. This conflict arises not only between socially constructed norms and inner wisdom, but also between the conscious ego and the fully developed and integrated self. Jung suggested that the best way out of these conflicts was to accept our destiny. By destiny he did not mean some fate over which there is no control. Rather it refers to Nature's plan for you. This plan is apparently embedded within one's individual constitution and is said to offer us the greatest possible self-fulfilment if only we can go along with it.

MASCULINITY VERSUS FEMININITY

Other conflicts can center on the masculine versus the feminine aspects of our psyche. This might be thinking versus feeling or rationalization versus intuition. Jung devel-

oped a system that he called functional types, in which he believed it is helpful to place oneself. It would be impossible to classify yourself as 100 percent within one category, but it may be a useful guide to help you to discover the conflicting aspects of your psyche and which parts may need more attention in order to achieve wholeness.

Jung distinguished four main functional types:

1. The thinking type. If you function most strongly in this domain, the area of thought and reason, then thinking is what Jung would call your "superior function" and you belong to the thinking type.

2. The intuitive type. This means that you know things in a direct intuitive way, sometimes with no need for rationalization.

3. The feeling type. This includes moral feelings as well as love and tenderness. In this case feeling needs to be separated from sensation, which is a physical thing.

4. The sensation type. This means that the superior way of functioning for you is in the domain of physical sensation.

If intuition is your superior function then sensation will tend to be inferior. If thinking is your superior function then feeling is likely to be inferior. Your inferior functions will need most work to enhance self-growth and help you become a more balanced person. Your dreams can be used to develop this process. If, for example, you are a scientist and a highly thinking type, then you can utilize your dreams to bring out the intuition that lies a little more hidden.

> # All the things one has forgotten
> ## scream for help in dreams.
>
> ELIAS CANETTI

The conflicts of life

Life can be viewed as nothing more than a series of conflicts. Without the experience of conflict and its accompanying pain, confusion, and catharsis, art, literature, and theater would be bereft. From Adam and Eve to the daily diet of soap opera dilemmas, conflict abounds. Some would argue that without conflict there is no living. Dreams of conflict are numerous and can take many different forms, from concrete dream images of battles and war, to more subtle scenarios of pain and tension. Not surprisingly, psychoanalytic thinkers and dream analysts have also turned their thoughts to conflict and how humans manage this life task.

Psychodynamic theorists believe that a person's behavior is determined by underlying psychological forces of which the person is unaware. These internal forces are thought to be dynamic—that is, they are constantly changing and readjusting and interacting with each other. This interaction is said to give shape to a person's thoughts, feelings, and behaviors. Symptoms or abnormal behaviors are said to emerge when conflicts occur between these psychic forces, or when the conflict is too painful and other behaviors unconsciously result from an attempt to lessen the pain.

A famous case involved Anna O, a patient treated by Freud and his colleague Josef Breuer. She had extensive symptoms of what at that time was called hysteria. This included paralysis of the legs, right arm, deafness, and disorganized speech. Breuer placed her under hypnosis in an attempt to cure her hysterical symptoms. However, while she was under the hypnosis she began to talk about her traumatic past events and she began to

express deeply felt emotions. This unleashing of repressed memories seemed to help the treatment. Anna O called this her talking cure. Breuer called it the cathartic method (a term that is derived from the Greek word *katharsis*).

Following this discovery, Breuer and his colleague Freud worked on a number of cases and together published a seminal text on this technique, *Studies in Hysteria*. In this they proposed that hysterical illnesses were caused by psychological conflicts of which the patient was not aware. They believed that these conflicts would produce a less negative influence on the sufferer once they had been raised into consciousness and brought into awareness. Over the following years Freud expanded this theory into a general theory of psychoanalysis. He argued that unconscious conflicts account not just for hysterical symptoms, but for all forms of normal and abnormal functioning.

Many theorists see life as a series of stages through which people must pass in a fixed order. Erik Erikson (1902–94), an ego psychologist, is one of the key psychological thinkers in this area and although he has been criticized, he has provided a comprehensive developmental theory in which life is divided into eight stages. Each stage is marked by a particular developmental crisis and a new set of drives and needs. The eight stages are: trust versus mistrust, autonomy versus shame and doubt, initiative versus guilt, industry versus inferiority, identity versus role confusion, intimacy versus isolation, generativity versus stagnation, and integrity versus despair. He suggested that abnormal behavior can appear at each developmental stage as a result of psychological inadequacy, biological abnormality, or extraordinary environmental stress. Successful resolution of each crisis can bring a person closer to ego identity. Unlike Freud, Erikson believed that the ego was strong enough to overcome any problems, and did not believe that a failure at any one stage would lead to arrested development.

Object relations theorists such as Melanie Klein, Margaret Mahler, Otto Kernberg, and Donald Winnicott focus on ideas of attachment versus separation as the central process in personality development. The motivating force in human behavior is thought to be the desire for relatedness, not the desire for instinctive gratification. The infant's early relationship with his or her caregiver is therefore the primary template for lifelong patterns of relatedness. They believe that people who have a "good enough" parenting experience progress effectively through developmental stages, each of which is characterized by separation and attachment issues.

TOP RIGHT: *Erik Erikson was an ego psychologist who specialised in the conflicts of life. One of his main theories was that human life is split up into eight key stages and each stage is marked by a particular development conflict.*

Conflict visualization

A simple visualization exercise can be useful in helping to understand all the ramifications of a conflicting situation. For example, try to imagine grappling with your own masked assassin. In the visualization try to make your assassin take off their mask to reveal another you. What does the other you look like? Notice how both of you feel and what you might have been afraid of. Try to make the fight turn benign and the weapon turn into cotton wool. How does it feel? In the end you find yourself in a game with your opponent. Which seems more natural—fighting or playing? How did the play end up? Notice how it was resolved, if at all.

Approach–avoidance conflict

Approach–avoidance conflict is said to be experienced when one is both drawn to and repelled by the same goal. It is usually incredibly difficult to resolve. A classic example is being offered a job with a large salary rise but also a substantial increase in workload. At a distance the ultimate reward of the salary rise seems desirable. However, on closer examination when you realize the extra commitment and responsibility that is required, the aversive qualities tend to dominate and hence the conflict becomes apparent. This can lead to a withdrawal from the situation, which in turn leads to an increase in the positive perception of the goal. Dreams of being stuck in a no-win situation, of being in a double bind, of never reaching the golden chalice, can tell of approach–avoidance conflicts.

Similarly, approach–avoidance conflict occurs when you have a conflict resulting from being repelled by two undesirable goals. There may be strong pressures upon you to chose either one or the other, but both seem equally unappealing. Another work-related example might be the conflict of choosing between being transferred to a different office in a different city and having to leave all your friends and family behind—but at least you still have a job. The alternative is being made redundant, where you lose your job but at least you are able to be near your friends and family. You may feel uninspired by both options and the conflict arises in your having to choose the lesser of two evils. Dreams associated with notions of control may tell of this kind of conflict. Such dreams might be connected to being trapped in a lift, being drowned with no escape route, or being held to ransom in some way. Often when such conflict is so intense you may chose to leave the field so as to prevent yourself from having to choose.

A variation on the approach–avoidance conflict is the double approach–avoidance conflict, or a case of chocolate cake versus carrot. Theorists suggest that this occurs when each of two goals have both a positive and a negative consequence. A useful example might be the conflict of someone who is on a diet being faced with the choice between a piece of chocolate cake versus a freshly peeled carrot. On the one hand the cake provides you with a delicious taste sensation, but thousands of calories. The carrot is by far the dieter's healthy option, but lacks the taste and excitement of the chocolate cake.

I had learned to see that the greatest and most important problems of life are all fundamentally insoluble. They must be so, because they express the necessary polarity inherent in every self-regulating system. They can never be solved but only outgrown...everyone must possess that higher level.

JUNG, *COMMENTARY ON THE SECRET OF THE GOLDEN FLOWER*, 1962

Conflict resolution vs. transcendence

The unconscious is said to be an efficient homeostatic system that is able to heal itself. When conflicts arise the balance can be reestablished. This is said to be done through the unconscious giving rise to symbols (often dream symbols) capable of reuniting conflicting tendencies which may seem irreconcilable on a conscious level. This capacity of the unconscious always fascinated Jung, who called it the transcendent function. He believed that although we may never be able to solve the most crucial conflicts or problems in life, we are able to transcend them.

Jung seems to be saying that a radical shift or wholeness occurs when one becomes fully aware of both poles of every conflict. This comes about through the power of the unconscious to create a new symbolical synthesis out of conflicting poles. It means that through our dreams the possibility of reconciliation between apparently irreconcilable forces is always there to be harnessed. Living with this in mind can bring great wisdom.

RIGHT: *There has long been an established link between Buddhism and Western psychotherapy, and in few places is this as pertinent as in the concept of transcendence. According to Shobogenzeo Genjo-koan (trans. Cook, 1985, p133): "To study the Buddha way is to study the self; to study the self is to forget the self; to forget the self is to be authenticated by the myriad things…" In spiritual terms, in becoming a true self we strive for unity between our conscious and unconscious, and in so doing transcend not only the egocentric self but the species as well. In psychological terms, when we transcend those limits we become more effective in concrete goals like work and family.*

CHAPTER 5

Anger

Rage can only with difficulty, and never entirely, be brought under the domination of the intelligence and is therefore not susceptible to any arguments whatever.

DREAMS THAT FEATURE SCENES OF ANGER, VIOLENCE, HOSTILITY AND AGGRESSIVENESS ARE

COMMON. MORE OFTEN THAN NOT THEY ARE SIGNS FROM YOUR UNCONSCIOUS THAT THERE IS

SOME UNACKNOWLEDGED AGGRESSION WITHIN YOU, BUT THEY MAY BE SIGNALING THAT YOU

NEED TO BE MORE AGGRESSIVE OR ASSERTIVE IN YOUR WAKING LIFE.

Understanding anger

UNCONSCIOUS ANGER

You may find that in your dreams, or even in your waking life, you display signs of road rage. Perhaps you get angry with shop assistants or waiting staff who ignore you or do not treat you in an adequate manner. Such behaviors are symptomatic of feeling undervalued and indicate that perhaps you are submissive in other more significant areas of your personal or social life. Unconscious hostile emotions are sometimes difficult to reach, as they are not really condoned in Western society and culture. The words aggression, hostility and anger generally carry negative and violent connotations. However, feelings of anger, when understood and managed thoughtfully, can be valuable emotions and can actually aid our personal growth and development. When such feelings emerge in our conscious and unconscious worlds, we can harness this energy to help us become more balanced as individuals who function within a wider context. Feelings of anger do not usually occur in isolation, but often are connected to other persons—either caused by them or by others who are the recipients of our anger. Dreams of anger therefore rarely happen without the presence of other dream characters.

AMBIVALENCE

The term ambivalence was introduced in 1911 by the psychiatrist Eugen Bleuler. The word is often used in day-to-day terms and in the vernacular to describe mixed feelings that you might hold about something or someone. However, Bleuler used the term to describe the coexistence of contradictory impulses and emotions toward the same object, which usually refers to the coexistence of feelings of love and hate. It means therefore much more than just not being sure or having mixed feelings. Ambivalence occurs when you simultaneously love and hate a person or thing. The contradictory attitudes emerge in response to the same source, whereas mixed feelings may be based on a realistic interpretation about the complexity or imperfect nature of something. Ambivalence is thought to be ingrained in all "neurotic" conflict.

PREVIOUS PAGE: *The words 'aggression', 'hostility' and 'anger' generally carry negative and violent connotations. Here in Hieronymous Bosch's work, which represents the Seven Deadly Sins being overseen by the eye of God, the Anger section depicts two men about to begin a jealous fight on a lawn in front of an inn. Anger in this manner usually occurs in connection with other persons—the emotion being caused either by them or by others who are the recipients of our anger. Dreams of anger therefore rarely happen without the presence of another person.*

Erica is so frightened by the power of her own mind and the content of the dream that she represses these thoughts and feelings even more.

Anger and loved ones

Experiences of hostility toward those you love or those who are closest to you are extremely common. In the world of dreams, this is also the case. It seems that we are able to let down our defenses with people we are close to and at some level perhaps we feel that they will be able to bear our feelings of aggression.

Erica's dream
Erica is a twenty one year old student who has had a spate of dreams concerning her father. In these dreams she sees her father being taken away and put on the guillotine. He is about to be killed when Erica wakes up in shock. She has had the same dream for several nights during the past week and she is deeply upset, shocked, and disturbed by it. At first glance this dream may not appear to be connected to feelings of anger or rage. However, in the light of Erica's current situation the link is more apparent. Erica is experiencing feelings of ambivalence and hostility toward her father for not supporting her through a new relationship and her career choice. She feels that he does not take her seriously and favors her younger sister. She has felt unable to express her anger toward him in words or in any other way because he is never available. He always seems to be busy with his high-powered job and she feels that the rest of the family would turn against her if she did say anything to him. Instead, her hostility toward him seems to come out in her dream of him being killed. Erica is so frightened by the power of her own mind and the content of the dream that she represses these thoughts and feelings even more. But they keep popping back up into her consciousness and probably will continue to do so until the issue is addressed to a satisfactory level for her.

Anger, conflict, and fighting

In psychoanalytic thinking, conflict refers to the opposition between apparently or actually incompatible forces. Internal or psychological conflict may be between instinctual impulses (e.g. libidinal and aggressive) or between structures (e.g. ego and id). The idea that all psychological conflict is neurotic is not part of psychoanalytic theory; conflicts are only neurotic if one party is unconscious and/or if they are resolved by the use of defenses other than sublimation.
Charles Rycroft, *The Critical Dictionary of Psychoanalysis*, 1995.

In dreams, episodes of conflict and associated feelings of anger take many guises. Conflict between what we want to do and what we think we should do are common occurrences in our dreams and can lead to feelings of frustration and aggressiveness, either within the dream or on waking. It is important to pay attention to the exact nature of our conscience or superego. In such cases, conflict dreams are usually dependent on our environment and upbringing and perhaps a dream of conflict is telling you of over-restrictive parenting.

Anger in a dream can refer to the tension between the conscious and unconscious ego. The aggressor in a dream, whether represented by you or some other character, will often represent the part of you that is demanding release from the depths of your unconscious. It may be that you are scared of releasing the emotion, but if you are able to acknowledge its strength, the power of the emotion can be harnessed in a positive way. Where there is unresolved inner conflict, there is often a tendency to project that emotion onto someone else.

Freud spoke of an aggressive drive which he said revealed itself in all walks of life and in all types of people. He believed that the aggressive drive was present as much in sex as in war. Freud argued in his later writing that aggression derived from the death instinct. Alfred Adler (1870–1937), an early disciple of Freud, believed that the aggressive power drive was the most fundamental force in the psyche. Aggressiveness can be sublimated, that is redirected into other energies. It can be redirected into sport, as in sports competitions. It can be redirected into sex, for making love, even when at its most tender, has an element of forcefulness within it. Aggressive tendencies and frustration can be redirected into problem-solving, artistic work, humor and comedy. People say that business is savage, because although the aggression is not physically expressed, entrepreneurial enterprise clearly involves an element of aggression.

RIGHT: *Many dream scenes depict the dreamer as an innocent victim of anger and aggression, such as in this extreme representation of the execution of Louis XVI , James Gillray's painting, **The Blood of the Murdered Crying For Vengeance.***

Personified anger exercise

If you have a dream in which feelings of anger are strongly apparent, try to visualize that emotion as a person—not necessarily someone you know, just a human. If the anger was expressed by a woman, what would she look like? How would she dress? How would she carry herself? What would her voice sound like? How would she smell? If the anger was expressed by a man, what would he sound like? How would you interact with him? What would you say to the personified anger? Could you have a conversation with him or her? What would you like to say? Try having a conversation with anger. How does it feel? What have you learnt from this exchange?

No man is angry that feels not himself hurt.

FRANCIS BACON

Dream weapons

If weapons appear in your anger dreams, it is worth considering your associations with them and what they might mean. The appearance of dream weapons may imply that you are immersed in powerful feelings of anger. Many dream weapons are connected to sexual imagery too, so it may be worth thinking about your sexual connections with the characters.

Anger without power is folly.   German Proverb

If you dream you are attacking a member of the opposite sex, take this seriously. Such a dream may reflect feelings of hostility that you have toward a specific other in your life or against that sex in general. It may also tell of your hatred of your own feminine/masculine side of your psyche and your dream may be showing how you would rather kill off than explore and come to value this side of yourself.

Many dream scenes can depict you as the victim of someone else's anger or aggression. The dream message here may be describing your feeling of being threatened—socially or at work. The dream would be signaling you to either get out while you can rather than bear the brunt of an attack, or else try to take on your attackers if you feel you can resist them. However, as it is also widely suggested that every item or aspect of your dream represents a part of you and your psyche, it could be worth trying to look for some part of you that you feel angry toward. Perhaps you are angry about some episode in the past and are harboring guilt feelings about it.

Guilt

The two feelings of anger and guilt are closely linked. Guilt is often derived from anger toward another person or situation. Anger quickly turns to guilt because the conscious may fear the overwhelming feelings of anger. Similarly anger can stem from unconscious feelings of guilt about an issue or person. According to classical psychoanalytic theory, guilt occurs as a consequence of the conflict between the superego and infantile sexual and aggressive wishes. In a sense the conflict between a child and his or her parents has become internalized and perpetuated. The complicating factor is that the superego is considered to gain its energy from the child's own aggression. The sense of guilt is therefore influenced by the extent to which a person expresses their aggressive feelings or internalizes them.

Animals and infants do not experience a sense of guilt, which is interesting to contemplate. They both experience anxiety, but not guilt. So the experience of guilt is based on the individual's capacity to internalize feelings. Only adult human beings with an awareness of others and time can experience guilt. All the psychological defenses that are used to reduce experiences of anxiety can be equally used to reduce experiences of guilt. But one defense, reparation, that is making good a perceived damage is used specifically to reduce feelings of guilt.

Dreams where feelings of guilt are experienced may be telling of repressed feelings of anger toward yourself and others. Dreams of anger may equally be connected to experiences of guilt, so be alert and be careful in your interpretations.

The guilty think all talk is of themselves.

GEOFFREY CHAUCER

Sc. 10 / Was zauderst du und hemmst den Todesstreich?
Johanna und Lionel, im Trauerspiel: Jungfrau von Orleans
gespielt von Dem. Schütz und Herrn Kunst.

Men vs. women on aggression

Mainstream thinking or common knowledge would have it that men are more aggressive than women. Men are believed to commit more frequent and extreme acts of violence than women. Throughout time and cultures women have largely been described as the gentle sex, free from hostility and anger. Yet the systematic psychological and sociological research in this area seems to suggest that it is not so clear-cut and that it all depends on a number of factors. In many situations women do behave in a less aggressive fashion than their male counterparts, but it has been suggested that this is due largely to the social and environmental expectations placed upon them and that when these are absent, women's aggressive tendencies become more obvious.

In 1979 three psychologists (Richardson, Bernstein, and Taylor) carried out an experiment to investigate this further. They brought together their experimental subjects and asked them to complete a reaction task in the lab. In the experiment female subjects were asked to compete with a fictional other on a reaction-time task. On each trial the subject is told that the slower of the two players will receive a small electric shock which the subject thinks is administered by their opponent—but in fact the experimenter determines this. The researchers classified their subjects into three different groups. In one group subjects took part in the study alone, with no one else was present or watching. In another group a female confederate was present as a silent observer. In the third group a female confederate was present but was allowed to offer verbal encouragement. The researchers expected that the subjects' inhibitions about being aggressive would be let down when they were in the private group. That is, they would show higher levels of aggression when alone than when someone else was with them. Indeed this proved to be the case. The women administered higher-level shocks to their opponents when they were alone. When another woman was egging them on their strength of shock was still fairly high. But when they were with a silent observer they toned down their aggression and the shocks given were at their lowest.

This experiment offered further support for the view that women's expression of aggression or anger is highly dependent on what they deem to be appropriate for their gender and place in a social setting. In replications of this experiment it has been found that women behave as aggressively as their male counterparts, although it does seem that the threshold before they reach this level of aggression is higher. When they are subjected to weaker provocation they seem to show lower levels of aggression. Women do, then, inhibit their aggressive feelings when they consider them to be inappropriate.

In terms of dream themes, this may lead us to conclude that without the inhibiting factor of waking consciousness and self censorship, women are likely to experience just as much aggression or anger in their dreams as their male counterparts—though the aggression may take different guises and may not be readily apparent.

LEFT: *Mainstream thinking would have it that men are more aggressive than women—the 'gentle sex'. However, at other times, it has been common for women to lead armies. At the time when Joan of Arc lived, expressions of aggression were not seen as incompatible with the female sex, and her leadership was not considered abnormal. Her leadership was so formidable that when she approached the English army at Patay, most of the English troops fled the battlefield in fear. Interestingly, Joan of Arc was encouraged in a dream to fight for the French against the English.*

Frustration and rage

Not to get what you have set your heart on is almost as bad as getting nothing at all. Aristotle.

Frustration dreams often take different guises and in these dreams you may be unaware of associated feelings of anger, but the two are related. Frustration generally describes the emotion experienced when you fail to achieve a goal of some sort. It is the deprivation that leads to the experience of frustration and the frustration can lead to anger and aggression. This can happen as much in waking life as in your dreams.

Joel's dream
Joel dreamt he was driving a brand new sports car around his local neighborhood on the way to collect his girlfriend. It was a hot summer day and Joel was driving with the roof down. He felt really proud of his new possession and was enjoying the attention that he was getting for it from passers-by. Suddenly Joel hit a massive traffic jam on a small road. He waited patiently but after five minutes of not moving he started to get frustrated. He began hooting his horn to see if it would make any difference, but to no avail.
Joel then decided in his dream that it would be easier to turn around and take another route to his girlfriend's place. He managed to turn in a drive, only to find that the traffic going the other way was just as bad and he was stuck for another ten minutes that seemed like hours. By this time Joel was incredibly frustrated and he ended smashing his car into the car in front. He reversed and did it again and again until his rage had in fact destroyed his own vehicle that he was so fond of. The phallic symbol of a new sports car is quite apparent in Joel's dream. Joel is not in a relationship and hasn't been for two years. He is feeling sexually frustrated. The appearance of the dream sports car and girlfriend may have contained an element of wish fulfilment. Joel's frustration at not being able to use the powerful vehicle properly leads to anger and self-destruction.

Rage can only with difficulty, and never entirely, be brought under the domination of the intelligence and is therefore not susceptible to any arguments whatever.
James Baldwin, *The Stranger in the Village* (1953), *Notes of a Native Son*, 1955.

Kohut (*The Search for the Self*, 1972) uses the phrase narcissistic rage to describe how those with narcissistic personality disorders react to dents on their self-esteem. In the term rage Kohut includes irritation to minor criticisms, to acts of vengeance carried out in cold blood. Humiliation and hate can be experienced in response to dents in the ego. Hate is confused with anger, but it could be argued that anger is a passing rather than an enduring emotion and hate is more embedded and closely connected to dents in the ego.

Catharsis

Catharsis is thought to be a useful way for managing aggression and our dreams may often tell of catharsis to help us to resolve uncomfortable conflict or manage painful emotions. The basic idea of catharsis is purging or letting off steam. It is thought that letting off steam can cause an angry person to feel better in some way and it can reduce their tendencies to get involved in dangerous acts of aggression. Social scientists have concluded that the catharsis hypothesis is not as simple as it seems. First, it does not happen as widely as we assume. Secondly, it is not always the case that when we vent our anger or even the score with someone against whom we feel aggrieved, this results in a happy ending. Our tendency to attack them on later occasions still remains.

Catharsis in dreams, fiction, plays and films abounds. Many fictional stories from Medea, through to Macbeth to your daily soap operas tell of conflict and anger between various characters and following a dramatic climax of rage, anger and purging of the soul, the key issues are resolved and everyone lives happily ever after. Look out for this the next time you watch television or go to the movies.

Catharsis may also happen in our dreams but it may in fact be more to do with wishful thinking than reality. That is not to say that complex feelings and issues cannot be resolved through talking, but it may not always be as simplistic and romantic as the movies sometimes portray.

Pete's dream

Pete had a tense relationship with his older sister, Eileen. There was always a lot of rivalry and competition between them and they used to joke about this at times. At other times the competition was fierce and spurred them both on to be high achievers academically and in their respective careers. In waking life Pete and his partner had just had their first child and were delighted. Pete's sister had not bought the baby a present and only came to visit once in the first six months even though she didn't live far away. One night Pete had a dream where he and Eileen had a major row in front of the whole family—grandparents, in-laws, and cousins. In the row Pete let out all his feelings of rage and he described the pain and anguish he felt about Eileen and her attitude. The family was watching silently. Eileen retaliated with her own rage. Everyone in the dream was hurt and distraught. At the end of the dream Pete's baby started to talk. Even though Pete could not actually understand the language and words, he knew that the infant was encouraging Pete and Eileen to resolve their differences. They did and the dream ended in harmony. In real life Pete had never been able to find the words to truly tell Eileen how he felt. He took this dream to be an encouragement to do this in a calm way before it got too late. Pete started the dialogue with Eileen and although reparations were slow and difficult at first, Pete realized that the dream had helped him to find a voice and to address his feelings of hostility in waking life.

LEFT: *In this 1886 painting of King Lear by George William Joy, the old king in prison is resolving his argument with his daughter, Cordelia who he had previously disinherited. The theme of catharsis features heavily in literature, and here in Shakespeare's* **King Lear** *following a dramatic climax of rage, the King eventually forgives Cordelia.*

CHAPTER 6

Death

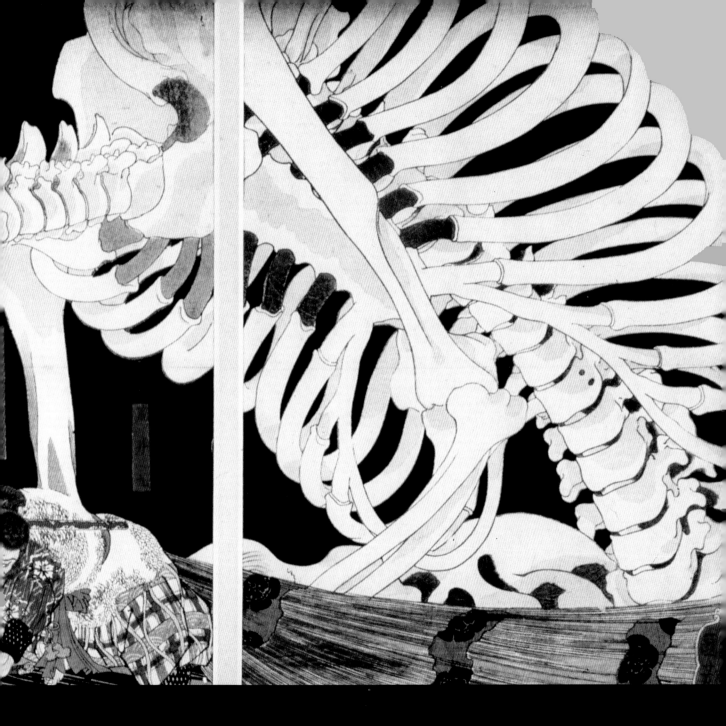

To be dead (in dreams) announces freedom from anxiety.

PERHAPS THE MOST PAINFUL AND POWERFUL EXPERIENCES OF OUR LIVES ARE OUR ENCOUNTERS WITH DEATH. NOT SURPRISINGLY, DREAMS OF DEATH AND DYING ARE FREQUENT AND VARIED, AND CAN HAVE MANY MEANINGS AND POSSIBLE INTERPRETATIONS. DREAMS OF DEATH ALWAYS NEED TO BE CAREFULLY AND SENSITIVELY EXAMINED AND THIS MUST ALWAYS BE DONE IN CONTEXT. FOR THE SAME DEATH DREAM MAY HAVE STRIKINGLY DIFFERENT INTERPRETATIONS FOR TWO DIFFERENT PEOPLE DEPENDING ON THEIR CURRENT AND PAST EXPERIENCES OF LIFE. FOR SOME PEOPLE DREAMS OF DEATH CAN BE FRIGHTENING AND RAISE ANXIETIES. FOR OTHERS DREAMS OF A DECEASED LOVED ONE CAN BE COMFORTING AND CAN EVEN PROVIDE GUIDANCE. EITHER WAY, IT IS IMPORTANT TO LOOK BEYOND THE INITIAL EMOTIONAL RESPONSE AND CONSIDER THE POSSIBLE MEANINGS THAT LIE BEHIND THE DREAM DEATH IMAGES. FOR IN FACT THEY MAY HERALD TIMES OF CHANGE, OF LEAVING THE OLD BEHIND, OR THEY MAY EXPRESS UNCONSCIOUS FEELINGS TOWARD SOMEONE CLOSE WHO IS LIVING.

War is not an adventure. It is a disease. It is like typhus.
Saint-Exupery, *Flight to Arras*, 1942.

From the First World War, Freud and others began to develop ideas about experiences of death, their connections to the dream world, and the development of the psyche. Freud was one of many practitioners at the time who bore witness to the horrific dreams of soldiers as they returned home from the trenches. He began to construct a theory that attempted to address their experiences—particularly in relation to their dreams. The main theories that Freud had to go on at that time—wish fulfilment or sexual symbolism—could not adequately explain the dreams of returning soldiers traumatized from battle.

PREVIOUS PAGE: *Dreams of death and dying that involve disturbing imagery such as Kuniyoshi Utagawa's* **Mitsukini's Defying the Skeleton Spectre** *are common. While often frightening, for some, dreams of deceased loved ones can be comforting as they provide an opportunity to "see" those closest to them again.*

Gestalt psychology

Fritz Perls, the founder of Gestalt psychology, insisted that dreams are about you and you alone. Perls suggested that in every single part of your dream a part of yourself or some aspect of your personality can be seen. In other words, other characters who may appear in your dreams are part of you and you should not try to kid yourself that they represent someone else. This thinking can be used to interpret dreams of death. In a death dream the person who has died or been murdered could well represent a part of your psyche. Perls would say that the dreamer needs to resist the temptation to explain away these dream characters as representations of other people. Rather we should look for their symbolism within our own minds and psychological functioning. For example, the appearance of a dream child is likely to represent aspects of your past that you feel you have lost and need to reintroduce into your conscious life. Similarly to dream of a person of the opposite sex dying may highlight the absence of the feminine or masculine within your psyche. The dream could be urging you to redress the balance.

Gestalt theories on dreams are not far removed from the thinking of Freud. Freud talked of the interaction that goes on between the id, the ego, and the superego. Gestalt psychologists would invite you to identify with each of these parts of yourself and pay attention to what each has to say rather than repress it.

A technique that was highly developed by Fritz Perls is largely based on the Jungian concept of active imagination. In this technique the Gestalt therapist may get a dialogue going between two key elements in a dream. They may be animals, objects or the deceased person and the living. Often they will use the two chairs exercise (see page 60) and play one character while you play the other. In a dream of death, for instance, the therapist might play you while you played the deceased. Then you might swap chairs while you take on the role of the other person. This move from chair to chair is intended to help people make the change from character to character. In this scenario, as the dead person you might find yourself telling the living of the joy of life and death and the wholeness that is achieved. As the living person you might tell the dead about your fears of dying, which may reveal the depth of your anxiety about dying.

Perls referred to these two roles as topdog and underdog. That is, one part of the dream dialogue stands for the conscious part of you, the side that is on show to yourself and the world at large. The other part of the dream is connected to the hidden part of your psyche that may be disgusting, or frightening in some way and is therefore repressed. Through this sort of dialogue, the underdog will find its voice, express its point of view, and accept its rightful place in you conscious life. Eventually the dialogue should lead to acceptance and agreement and wholeness of the various parts of your mind.

Perls himself was not keen to use the term unconscious, but preferred to talk about that part of the mind that is hidden from view. Like Jung, he believed that the process of integration was the main task of the dream. He also believed that when telling the story of your dream you should do it in the present tense to actually relive it. So you would say "I am standing at my mother's funeral. I am watching the people walking by her grave. I am upset but I am unable to cry…" In this way it is alive and real to you. It is not something unrelated or external. Your dreams, therefore, reflect something in your present state of anxiety. These anxieties may be connected to something in your childhood, but can be dealt with in the here and now.

As with most theories on dreams it is up to you to decide which parts are useful and which are not. It may be that we dream easily of people whom we encounter in everyday life and that dreams of these people have no greater meaning for us than a simple surface one. On the other hand, perhaps many more dreams than we give credit for are actual representations of our internal world and make reference to our unconscious.

Life-death instinct

As a result of his encounters with First World War veterans, Freud started to wonder whether aggression, as well as sex, might be an important instinct that is prone to repression and therefore liable to lead to neurosis. In 1920 his thinking led him to develop a new theoretical framework within psychoanalysis. In *Beyond the Pleasure Principle* (1920) Freud introduced the concept of a death instinct. According to Freud's theory, there are two basic instincts, a life instinct or Eros and a death instinct or Thanatos. Later writers termed the death instinct *mortido* or *destrudo*. The life instinct essentially is made up of the old part of the libido or sex drive and is said to be part of the drive that we all have toward self-preservation. The death instinct, however, is something quite separate from the libido and is said to represent an innate human drive to self-destruction. Whereas the life instinct is a creative force for self-development, preservation, and survival, the death instinct on the other hand is said to drive us toward death and the ultimate state of complete freedom from tension or anxiety or struggle.

On the basis of this theory Freud suggested that war itself could be a nation's attempt at directing its aggression outward rather than inward to avoid self-destruction through internal battles. Similarly suicide in this framework can be seen as a failure to preserve oneself, that is anger is so strongly turned in on the self that it leads to self-destruction. Dreams of suicide are by no means predictive and can have many interpretations. If you commit suicide in the dream it would probably indicate that you no longer feel able to cope with a certain situation, perhaps you are frustrated, looking for a solution or a way out. If you witnessed someone else's suicide it may be that some aspect of yourself is feeling neglected. It is worth considering how the other person interacts with you within the dream and what parts of that person you identify with. Alternatively you may be harboring unconscious feelings of anger toward that person.

As with suicide, less severe but self-destructive acts can also be seen in this same light. Unconscious and self-destructive forces are at play in all that we do—unconsciously motivated accidents, self-inflicted diseases, secret offenses committed with the unconscious intent of wanting to be caught. Dreams of accidents are often significant and are less accidental than we actually may think. They may tell of an unconscious anger, envy or rage against the person who had the accident. Alternatively, the dream person may represent an aspect of your self that you have repressed for various reasons. Even if the accident happened to someone in the dream whom you believe you are very close to and are fond of, think carefully about your real feelings toward them as you may be harboring feelings of animosity that could be addressed in waking life.

Many of Freud's theories about death and dreams were criticized at the time and still are today. Most contemporary psychoanalysts accept Freud's account of aggression and its implications, although they usually make little reference to Freud's notions of earlier life and death instincts.

RIGHT: *In the 19th century Spanish painter Leonardo Alenza's piece* **The Suicide,** *a man is about to throw himself off a cliff in a desperate act of suicide. While dreams of suicide are not predictive, they have many interpretations including not being able to cope with a certain situation, frustration or the search for a way out.*

Katie is a twelve-year-old girl who has regular dreams about her brother being killed in a hurricane. She wakes just before he is about to die but is terrified on waking. Katie and her family were in fact involved in a hurricane just last year and although no one was killed, the whole episode was highly distressing for her. Because of the upheaval and family upset, Katie felt unable to talk to anyone about her fears and fantasies that it might happen again. These dreams were perhaps a way of her unconscious letting her know that her anxieties needed to be addressed. After a long spate of these night terrors, Katie's parents were finally able to put their own practical and financial concerns on the back burner and began to listen to Katie's innermost fears and feelings of guilt. They helped Katie express her worries through talking and poetry, which she enjoyed writing. After just a few days the nightmares about death completely stopped.

There is a constant need to deal with the aggression in a way that is least destructive to the individual.

Repetition compulsion

Freud believed that repetition compulsion clearly revealed itself in the battle dreams of the First World War soldiers. He suggested that these repetitive dreams were related to the death instinct and its tendency to force us to return to earlier states. That is, since the animate develops out of the inanimate, there is equally an innate drive, the death instinct, which drives us to return to our inanimate state.

Psychiatrists and biologists at that time and up to the present day strongly dispute this and have suggested that repetitive dreams such as these that follow a traumatic event, function to help the mind to assimilate the disturbing and initially intolerable information, with the ultimate aim of aiding integration.

THE PLEASURE PRINCIPLE

The term pleasure principle is perhaps misleading, as it implies that pleasure is positively sought. In fact Freud seemed to be saying that it is a case of displeasure being actively avoided. For example, it is generally unpleasurable and also potentially dangerous for aggression to be turned inward onto the individual. So there is a constant need to deal with the aggression in a way that is least destructive to the individual. Freud suggested that this could be achieved in two ways: first by eroticizing it—combining it with the libido—in which case it may take the form of masochism or sadism; or secondly by directing the aggression outward in the form of aggression against others.

Individuation

Jung on death

I dreamed that my wife's bed was a deep pit with stone walls. It was a grave and somehow had a suggestion of classical antiquity about it. Then I heard a deep sigh, as if someone were giving up the ghost. A figure that resembled my wife sat up in the pit and floated upwards. It wore a white gown into which curious black symbols were woven. I awoke, roused my wife, and checked the time. It was three o'clock in the morning. The dream was so curious that I at once thought it might signify a death. At seven o'clock came the news that a cousin of my wife had died at three o'clock in the morning.

C.G. Jung, *Memories, Dreams and Reflections*, 1963.

For Jung, birth, death, life, and rebirth all featured as part of the individuation process. This process is essentially the development of the psyche into its full stage of maturation and harmony. In Jungian terms, to dream of a birth may tell of a new phase in your personal development. A dream of death therefore may signal the actual or emotional end of a phase, or way of being. Jung would emphasize the importance of working on dreams of death, since they usually herald the end of an era of some sort—the giving up of a negative attitude, the loss of an old emotion, anxiety or feelings of guilt.

Jung called the final of four stages of individuation complete self-realization, and he proposed that not many people got this far in their life cycle. In this stage we are said to encounter what Jung called the self. He distinguished between the ego, which he thought of as the conscious mind, and the self, which he considered to be the total, fully integrated psyche. All the opposing and conflicting elements of the psyche are united within the self. In the final stage, those aspects of the self that were opposites become united and whole. Our dreams of death can facilitate this process, as they can take us on a journey through our unconscious worlds to enable full integration of the psyche. In this stage of realization we are said to know

RIGHT: *Many Native Americans believe that in our dreams we encounter a spiritual guide. Here in Frederic Remington's painting* The Vision, *the Native American soldier's guide appears in front of him.*

truth or reality. We do not consciously reason with issues, neither do we sit and fantasize, we just know. Jung described this state:

This widening consciousness is no longer that touchy, egotistical bundle of personal wishes, fears, hopes and ambitions which always has to be compensated or corrected by unconscious counter-tendencies; instead it is a… relationship to the world of objects, bringing the individual into absolute binding and indissoluble communion with the world.

Jung believed that this stage of individuation was similar to the state of higher consciousness that can be achieved through meditation—what some people call God or The One in Eastern traditions. Your beliefs about life, death, and life after death will be reflected through your death dream images.

Jung has been criticized for being too rigid in his four-stage theory of individuation. He also claimed every uninterrupted dream had four parts to it—setting the scene, defining the problem, moving toward a climax, and solution to the problem. You will need to judge for yourself if his ideas are useful to you. However, a dream symbol may tell you what direction to follow to help yourself in the next stage of self realization.

Death dream exercise

It can be useful to focus your mind on what life will be like after your death and to visualize a familiar scene without your presence. You could picture your funeral and how you would like it to be. Some people even enjoy imagining what would be written in their own epitaph. This may sound morbid, but acceptance of death can help us to get a sharper focus on the task of living.

...an old man who cannot bid
farewell to life appears as sickly
as a young man who is unable
to embrace it.

C. G. JUNG

Resurrection scenes

Any death or resurrection symbolism may tell of the descent of the conscious ego into the unconscious and of the reemergence as a new transformed being. Such scenes may include straightforward death images, flooding and renewal, sunset followed by sunrise, the kiss of life, and the raising of a corpse. Whether this means that you are currently at the end of a process of realization or that you are being invited to embark upon a journey is hard to tell and must be left up to your own judgment.

Jung's last years continued to focus on his process of "becoming." At the age of eighty-two he began writing his autobiography with the words "My Life is a story of the self realization of the unconscious." His interest in the world seemed to broaden rather than narrow down in his later years. He developed a fascination with UFOs and a worry about the future of the species, which is highly evident in his book The Undiscovered Self (1958). It seemed that for Jung, ageing was not just the shortening of life; it was a process of refinement—"shrinking in death only robs the second half of life of its purpose." Jung believed in the possibil-ity of life after death but was not adamant about it. He did believe in the archetypal assumption that we survive after our death. He said that this is not only found in dreams, but that a belief in some form of afterlife is the universal belief across cultures. Jung's faith in the archetype combined with his quest for understanding kept him going until he was eighty-five years old, in June 1961. At this time he had two strokes within two weeks and died surrounded by his family. His last words to his housekeeper, Ruth Bailey, were apparently: "Let's have a really good red wine tonight" (Vincent Brome, Jung—Man and Myth, 1978).

Michaela's dream
Michaela frequently has dreams about her mother and father, both of whom died when she was young. Far from being frightened by these dreams, she sees them as a comfort, as a positive communication from the two special people in her life. Often these dreams occur at times of stress or decision-making. Recently her father appeared to Michaela in a dream just a couple of days before she had an important job interview. Michaela awoke from the dream upset because she realized again how much she missed his presence and guidance. At the same time she felt pleased to have spoken to him. She believed that her father was trying to encourage her in this change of direction in life, with a new career and lifestyle. Even though Michaela had doubts about whether it was the right thing, she felt reassured by his dream comments to her.

LEFT: *Abraham Lincoln has long been credited by paranormalists with having supernatural powers. Before his assassination in 1865, Lincoln was believed to have had a prophetic dream about a coffin surrounded by weeping mourners who said that the President had been assasinated. Lincoln saw his face distorted in a mirror: "I noticed that one of the faces was a little paler, say five shades, than the other". Freud believed that this 'death instinct' represents an innate human drive to self-destruction.*

Sometimes joyous occasions like a wedding or a birth can tell us of feelings of loss as one era of our life ends to introduce the beginnings of a new one.

Repressed feelings

RITES OF PASSAGE

Dreams of funerals, or other rites of passage that may not be connected with death, can tell the dreamer of the passing of time and unconscious experiences of loss. Sometimes joyous occasions like a wedding or a birth can tell us of feelings of loss as one era of our life ends to introduce the beginnings of a new one. In such dreams it can be helpful to identify the characters within the dream and notice what they symbolize. Dreams of funerals and funeral paraphernalia, such as tombstones, graveyards, and grave diggers, can reflect the dreamer's own anxiety about the passing of time. Burials may be quite concrete metaphors for something that is buried or repressed within the psyche.

MURDER

Dreams of murder also tell of unconscious and repressed resentments or feelings of hostility. If you were being murdered in the dream, notice who was murdering you. As the Gestalt psychologists would say, a dream of murder may represent an aspect of your self that has been hidden away but is now fighting for your attention. If you were the murderer, the dream may point to hostility toward someone or yourself. You may have unconscious aggression toward a parent or dominant figure in your life. The anger may result from sibling rivalry that is manifesting itself in your dream life, and requires your attention. Alternatively you may be trying to kill off or hide an aspect of your psyche. If this is the case then your dream of murder could be a warning to examine these feelings before it is too late.

RIGHT: *Jaques-Louis David's depiction of murder shows the assassinated leader of the French Revolution, Jean Paul Marat. Marat was killed whilst in his bath tub by a young Royalist, Charlotte Corday. In dreams where you are being murdered, try to remember to see who your assassin was. Murder can represent feelings that have been hidden away. However, if you were the killer in your dream, this points towards hostility toward yourself or someone else.*

Du 13 Juillet, 1793
Marie ann Charlotte
Corday au citoyen
Marat.
Il suffit que je sois
bien Malheureuse
pour avoir Droit
à votre bienveillance.

À MARAT,
DAVID.

CHAPTER 7

Joy & Sa

Your joy is your sorrow unmasked. The self same well from which your laughter rises was oftentimes filled with your tears.

KAHLIL GIBRAN

ness

MOST PEOPLE'S MOODS ARE GENERALLY TRANSIENT. FOR A PERIOD OF TIME WE MAY FEEL A LIGHTNESS AND JOY ABOUT OURSELVES AND THE WORLD, BUT BEFORE WE KNOW IT THIS SEEMS TO VANISH BEFORE OUR VERY EYES AND WE BECOME BURDENED AND WEIGHED DOWN BY EVENTS, RESPONSIBILITIES, AND THE PERCEPTIONS WE HOLD ABOUT OURSELVES AND OUR WORLD. OUR DREAMS CAN PROVIDE US WITH A DEEP AND POWERFUL INSIGHT INTO OUR MOODS AND CAN BE USED TO HELP US MANAGE MOODS AND FEELINGS OF JOY AS WELL AS FEELINGS OF SADNESS.

Our dreams can create their own emotions of sadness or joy, and they can be explored with this in mind. Sometimes we awake overcome by feelings of sadness and melancholia that we know are associated to our dream experience, but we do not necessarily remember the dream or understand the message it conveys. At other times, the narrative is very clear and we remember feeling distressed by a particular event in our dream, such as the death of a friend or a terrible natural disaster. As in our waking life, it is sometimes easy to make connections between an actual event or person, and at other times it is as though we cannot find a clear way through to understanding our emotions at all. Despite this, it is important to try and remember how you felt and to make connections to those same feelings in your waking life. This will help you to become more familiar with your emotional responses, in the same way that you might seek to know your physical body and learn to respond to areas of pain and vulnerability.

Equally important are those dreams which inspire feelings of euphoria and unexplained happiness. Many people know the experience of waking up from a dream laughing without really knowing why. These feelings of immense joy and happiness are just as important to understand as sadness is for, again, they allow us to focus in on the real life experiences and situations that evoke them.

Emotions of joy and sadness are undoubtedly dependent on the external world in which we live as well as our psychological and biological makeup. Situations that make people feel sad and depressed today may be very different from those situations that made people feel sad ten years ago. There also may be striking differences between what men and women feel sad about. The social constructions of both joy and sadness are important to bear in mind when analyzing dream emotions. Dreams can reflect the numerous ways in which people feel about themselves.

Feelings of sadness or what we commonly term depression seem to have captured society's imagination from the earliest of times. The Old Testament speaks of the severe depression of Moses, Saul, and Nebuchadnezzar. Queen Victoria of England and Abraham Lincoln are thought to have experienced repeated bouts of depression. Similarly artists and musicians such as George Frederick Handel, Sylvia Plath, Ernest Hemingway, Eugene O'Neill, and Virginia Woolf are thought to have been plagued by experiences of depression.

PREVIOUS PAGE: *This painting, the* **Gloria Triptych** *by Guiseppe Mentessi, accurately depicts the intensity of feelings of joy and sadness. In the first segment, a woman kisses her beloved child, whilst the second depicts a tumultous event taking place which displaces the woman's happiness. In the third, we see the woman mourning her loss with the same depth of feeling with which she was able to express joy.*

Depression and dreams

Woke at one, and lay melancholy till three or four—then sleeping, only to dream of finding a dead body of a child in a box, a little girl whom I had put living into it and forgotten.
John Ruskin, *Diaries*, February 24, 1885.

So much psychological terminology has entered popular culture and language over the past fifty years that people who often feel low or more dejected than normal refer to themselves as being depressed. In many instances they are describing normal mood swings, a response to difficult or sad life events, or an understandable level of fatigue or unhappy thoughts.

Some medical practitioners, however, become annoyed when this term is bandied about, because within medicine the word depression refers to a clinical syndrome. This is a severe psychological disturbance accompanied by longstanding psychological pain. It is so debilitating that a clinically depressed person may be unable to function or may even try to take their life. If you are feeling this way, then you might want to seek professional guidance. For the purpose of this book the vernacular term depression in the sense of sadness rather than its clinical counterpart will be used.

We can often awake from a dream with a real sense of sadness and sometimes tearfulness. Sometimes the reasons for this are clear from the dream. Perhaps you find yourself dreaming about a deceased loved one, for example. On other occasions, however, you may not be able to remember what it was that made you so sad. In fact the sorrow may emerge from some unconscious feelings about something in your waking life. If a dream of sadness or sorrow recurs you should take it seriously, particularly if you are feeling depressed in your waking life.

One cloud is enough to eclipse all the sun.
Thomas Fuller M.D., *Gnomologia*, 1732.

Dreams of blackness, clouds, darkness, and struggle of some kind can all symbolize feelings of sadness, oppression, and depression. Take note of these dreams and the emotion experienced in any dream, because whatever their contents are they can all provide tell-tale clues as to what may be going on in your unconscious.

Martin's dream
Martin awoke from his last dream with tears in his eyes and yet at the same time he felt delighted and overjoyed despite the apparent sadness. He felt paralyzed for a moment and then slowly started to consider the content of his dream. He dreamt that he had been watching the most exciting and energetic performance of the musical West Side Story. It was so real to him. He watched all the dancers and knew all the moves. It even felt as though he was singing along to the songs in his dream.

He was in the audience and wanted to go and congratulate the lead actress, but was paralyzed and unable to get out of his seat. He felt frustrated but mostly sad that he would not get to speak with her and connect with her in any way. At the same time he felt thrilled by the show. On reflection Martin realized that this dream might relate to his partner, who had traveled to the United States last week for a promotion. Martin was elated about this change in career and realized it was a good move for them both. But at the same time he felt sad about this loss. Both of these feelings combined with the difficulties of being apart are represented in this dream scene.

Dreams of flying, playing, and ascending are often connected to feelings of joy and happiness.

Happiness

A string of excited, fugitive, miscellaneous pleasures is not happiness; happiness resides in imaginative reflection and judgement, when the picture of one's life or of human life, as it truly has been or is, satisfies the will, and is gladly accepted.
George Santayana, *Persons and Places: The Middle Span*, 1945.

Sometimes we may experience feelings of extreme joy and elation in our dreams. Dreams of flying, playing, and ascending are often connected to feelings of elation, joy and happiness. Flying dreams can evoke and represent feelings of freedom and liberation—breaking away from the shackles that bind us. Flying dreams can also tell of a movement toward your authentic or true self. They may symbolize a period of creativity for you or even excitement and joy about your waking world or what lies ahead. Dreams of laughter, however, may not always be what they seem and can hold a more sinis-

ter side to them. Sometimes we may be laughing at something that seems stupid or ridiculous and not particularly funny. At other times that laughter can conceal emotions of humiliation or even aggression. It is important to consider the context of the laughter or joy in your dream before you decide on its meaning.

RIGHT: *Flying dreams can represent feelings of freedom and liberation—getting rid of the shackles that bind us—and of a movement toward our authentic or true selves.*
***This painting,* Attempted Flight by Winged Men** *captures the often-surreal quality of flight dreams.*

Visualization

To prompt dreams of joy you could try embarking on visualization exercises during the day and see whether your dream life is affected. One such task would be to look for flying objects during the day. These might be leaves, seeds, insects, birds, planes, or even kites. Then try to imagine the world as it looks from their perspective. Notice how the world looks and what you can see from above the ground. How does it feel and what do all the people look like? Tell yourself that you will be able to fly in your dreams that night. Imagine yourself when you are asleep and then visualize your dream body rising out of your sleeping body and then taking itself out through an open window into the sky to go on an exciting and joyous journey. Observe what your dream body sees on its travels and how it feels. If you do dream of flying that night, remember how it feels and try to take some guidance from the dream.

Melancholia

Freud used the term melancholia to talk about the condition that we now call depression. Freud concluded that melancholia existed when the ego is in mourning for somebody or something that has been denied or lost. He said this occurs when emotional investment, energy or libido in that person has been withdrawn, then the ego identifies itself: "I cannot have you any longer for myself so I will become myself." Freud considered that the lost object or person becomes a bad object because otherwise the loss would be too unbearable. Freud connects this to the overwhelming level of denigration and despair which is so prevalent in experiences of depression. By extension, if contact with the external world ceases, then this despair would be heightened and intensified by delusions of punishment or self-destruction. He therefore concluded that suicide in the context of depressive illness represents the killing of the ego by the self at the command of the superego.

MANIA OR ELATION

The few psychoanalytical studies of mania suggest that it is the reverse of depression. It is suggested that elation occurs when the ego feels that it has triumphed over or become fused with the superego, and instead of feeling depressed and alienated it feels liberated and at one with the world. Dreams where extreme happiness is experienced can be considered within this context. As well as considering ideas about wish fulfilment, it may be worth noticing whether some psychic struggle has been going on that you feel may have been realized in your unconscious dream world.

IT'S DEPRESSING FOR WOMEN

Is anyone in the world / Safe from unhappiness? Sophocles, *Oedipus at Colonus*, 401 B.C.

Research shows that more women are diagnosed with depression than men. Many explanations and theories have tried to explain why this might be the case. Some theorists say that culture is constructed in such a way that it permits women to display their emotions, while depressed men may turn to drink or violence instead. Others maintain that there is a genetic component. Psychoanalytic theorists attribute this divide to penis envy. They suggest that women suffer low self-esteem as a result of their lifetime longing to have a penis and are more vulnerable to loss and depression.

Other theorists suggest that women's devalued role in society makes them more vulnerable and prone to depression. Edvard Munch was inspired by his depressed sister, Laura, to paint the picture *Evening, Melancholy: On The Beach*. Dodie Smith, the author of the best-selling book *One Hundred and One Dalmations*, said that "Noble deeds and hot baths are the best cure for depression" (*I Capture the Castle*, 1948).

Splitting

It might now be useful to consider the defense mechanism known as splitting. The process of splitting has been described by psychoanalysts as a means by which the difficulties or stress that are experienced can be compartmentalized. The positive and the negative aspects of others are completely separated. When splitting occurs, there is a tendency to view oneself and others in polar opposites, switching back and forth between highly positive and extremely negative images. In our dream worlds this process can reveal itself in different guises. We may dream of angels and devils, of black and white, of good and evil. If these types of dream images are appearing or you find yourself dividing the world into good and bad then it may be worth taking time to consider what these defenses may mean. It may be that you are trying to protect yourself from some kind of psychic pain.

LEFT: *Blake's painting,* **Good and Evil Angels Struggling for the Possession of a Child,** *depicts good and evil forces in conflict over an innocent. It illustrates well the dream defence mechanism known as splitting, where the dreamer splits good from bad to make the stress of the dream easier to deal with.*

The notion of wish fulfilment is always with us and often reveals itself in our dreams when our defenses are down.

The pleasure principle

Freud proposed that initially when we are infants the psyche functions solely in relation to the pleasure principle or the pleasure–pain principle. In this the aim of the psyche is to avoid pain. Later in life, once the ego has developed, the pleasure principle is modified by the reality principle. The reality principle leads the individual to replace hallucinatory wish fulfilment with adaptive behavior. But the notion of wish fulfilment is always with us and often reveals itself in our dreams when our defenses are down.

In psychoanalysis wish fulfilment is thought to be a complex process where instinctive or id impulses are satisfied and, as a result, psychic tension is reduced. In classical Freudian thinking dreams are thought to be vehicles for wish fulfilment. In dreams the id fails to notice any difference between fantasies, hallucinations or images and reality, so the dreamer can develop full and complex wishes in their dreams that would not be allowed to seep through to consciousness in waking life.

Although this theory is quite complex and can be confusing, on another level our dreams can quite simply and concretely reflect our unconscious wishes in an obvious way. For example, if you are feeling burnt out at work and wanting to escape, you may dream that you are on a warm desert island somewhere with nothing to worry about. If you are attracted to a member of the opposite sex in waking life, you may dream of a romantic encounter with that person. If you have money worries in waking life, you may dream of winning the lottery. If you are concerned about the ageing process, you may dream of yourself as a young child. It is important to remember that this is just one explanation and that the meaning of your dreams will be individual to you. However much a dream may tell you about a simple wish fulfilment, it is still necessary to consider its imagery as there may be a multitude of layers to uncover in determining its actual explanation.

Rikki's dream
Rikki has a recurrent dream that he wins the lottery and the same numbers appear to him each time he plays in his dream. He wins millions and uses it to treat all his friends to a massive holiday abroad. He is concerned about this dream and wonders if it is predictive, so in waking life he actually buys a lottery ticket. He doesn't win. When you know Rikki's background and life circumstances, this dream appears to be more complicated than it initially seems. Rikki is a teenager who has been brought up in care homes for all his life. He finds it incredibly difficult to trust people and rarely talks about his thoughts and feelings to anyone. He just tries to block them out and gets on with living life to the full. He has been deprived of all of life's emotional and physical comforts and is longing to feel secure and loved by those around him. This dream seemed to express these feelings in images rather than words.

Learned helplessness

Many psychological theorists connect experiences of depression to something they have termed learned helplessness. This concept is something akin to a loss of control.

Mel's dream

Mel's dream seems to be a direct reflection of her perceived reality. In the dream she sees herself as she does in her waking life, as an unattractive, unsociable college student. She feels unable to hold down basic waitressing jobs and believes that she will fail to get her degree and will be absent from the graduation ceremony. In the past these feelings of inadequacy had caused her to leave college and drop-out. She feared this would happen again and a sense of inevitability accompanies this emotion.

According to Martin Seligman and his colleagues such feelings of loss of control lie at the center of Mel's depression. Since the mid-1960s Seligman has been developing the learned helplessness theory of depression, which combines ideas from cognitive and behavioral theories. It suggests that when people become depressed they feel that they no longer have control over the reinforcements in their lives and that they are themselves responsible for this helpless state.

Dreams of loss of control may signal unconscious feelings that lie within the psyche and are worth listening to, as they could prevent further difficulties in waking life. Loss of control dreams may be connected to cars, trains, planes, and boats veering out of control. They may be linked to drowning in deep waters. They could be connected to losing control in public in some way. They could even be dreams of being unable to control your speech or means of expression. That is not to say that all dreams of loss of control herald the onset of a period of depression, rather that it is worth noting the context of the dream and the element of control within it. Such dreams may signal an internal psychological shift that you fear or would prefer to keep repressed, rather than an external life change.

SELIGMAN'S EXPERIMENT

Seligman used animals to test his theory of learned helplessness. He and his colleagues were trying to teach dogs to escape and then avoid shocks. They placed each dog in a shuttle box—a box divided by a low barrier for the dog to jump over. They dimmed the lights to try to warn the dogs that something was about to happen and then they administered a series of small electric shocks. The shocks continued until the dog learned to avoid them by jumping over the barrier. Before they did this experiment, Seligman and his team let some of the dogs rest the day before (called naïve dogs). Others had spent the previous day strapped into equipment in which they received inescapable shocks at random. The naïve dogs learnt how to escape from the shocks after a while and placed themselves in the shock-free part of the shuttle box. The other set of dogs had a different reaction, though. When the shock was first administered they would run around the box frenetically, but after a while they gave up and lay down and whined. Even when the shock was turned off they just lay there. The next time the shock was administered they did the same thing. They seemed to give up: "at first it struggled a bit, and then after a few seconds, it seemed to give up and accept the shock passively. On all succeeding trials, the dog failed to escape. This is the paradigmatic learned helplessness finding" (Seligman, *Helplessness*, 1975).

The assumption in both disciplines is the same—that is anything uncertain or unknown is filled by the observer's own projections.

Alchemy

In later life Jung further developed his strong interest in alchemy. His thinking around this subject provides useful material for understanding joy and sadness and their relation to our dream worlds. Jung concluded that the ancient tradition of alchemy attempted to make sense of a universally valid truth—that is, that one becomes aware of new meanings within the unconscious by seeing them mirrored in outer reality. He suggested that alchemy was based on sound principles that were connected with the psychological phenomenon of projection.

In 1944 he published *Psychology and Alchemy* in which he reported a series of dreams of a natural scientist who had no knowledge of alchemy. He illustrated the resemblance between the dreams and the alchemical texts. Like the analytical psychology of Jung, alchemy represented a discipline promoting self-realization. The assumption in both disciplines is the same—that is, anything unknown is filled by the observer's own projections. In the case of unknown dreams it is your own associations and projections that will create the best meaning for you. Jung developed stages of the alchemical opus and related them to his own beliefs about the individuation process. The nigredo (blackening or initial stage) is to do with depression.

RIGHT: *Jung believed that the ancient tradition of alchemy was based on principles connected with the psychological phenomenon of projection—placing our own unknown and unfulfilled desires onto another person or thing—which is so often at work in our dreams.*

CHAPTER 8

Love looks not with the eyes, but with the mind;
And therefore is winged Cupid painted blind.

WILLIAM SHAKESPEARE

OUR MOST INTIMATE RELATIONSHIPS ARE FREQUENT AND FERTILE SUBJECT MATTER FOR OUR DREAMS. WHETHER RELATED TO PARENTS, CHILDREN, FRIENDS OR LOVERS, OUR DREAM WORLDS ARE SATURATED WITH THE JOY, FRUSTRATION, AND SUBTLE COMPLEXITIES THAT LIE AT THE CORE OF THE HUMAN EXPERIENCE KNOWN AS LOVE. DREAMS OF RELATIONSHIPS ARE USUALLY CONNECTED TO UNCONSCIOUS AND CONSCIOUS EXPERIENCES OF LOVE AND OFTEN APPEAR IN DIFFERENT GUISES. BY ANALYZING UNCONSCIOUS DREAM LOVE MESSAGES, WE HAVE THE POWER TO DISCOVER THE HIDDEN TRUTHS THAT CAN HELP US NEGOTIATE WAKING RELATIONSHIPS WITH MORE EASE. THE COMPLEX CLUSTERS OF FEELINGS AND EMOTIONS THAT COMBINE TO CREATE THE NOTION OF "LOVE" HAVE SEEPED INTO SOCIAL CONSCIOUSNESS AND CULTURES ACROSS THE WORLD. IN ITS ATTEMPTS TO UNDERSTAND THE MEANINGS OF LOVE AND ITS SYMBOLISM WITHIN OUR DREAM WORLDS, THE SCIENCE OF PSYCHOLOGY HAS BEEN INFLUENCED BY LITERATURE AND PHILOSOPHY AS WELL AS ANCIENT MYTHOLOGY.

Psychology of love

Psychologists have struggled over the years to try to define and develop theories of love. Many of them argue that the study of love is better left to poets and artists. Love dreams are therefore often assumed to be confusing, and their analysis is usually complex. In *Contributions to the Psychology of Love* (1910) Freud made the observation that the field of love had been "left to the creative writer to depict for us the 'necessary conditions' for loving." The British psychoanalyst Charles Rycroft was equally confused about the concept of love and said that psychoanalysis had "as much difficulty in defining this protean concept as elsewhere."

Despite this confusion, psychologists and others generally define love as (1) an intense feeling of liking or affection and (2) an enduring sentiment toward a person with a strong desire to be with that person. In our dreams, however, sexual fantasies and imagery are often more readily depicted than the more ephemeral images of love. Through the interpretation of

the dreams of individual patients, Freud used this aspect of the unconscious to develop a range of theories about sex and sexual energy rather than love itself. Freud's ideas about sexual expression have been absorbed into most aspects of dream analysis.

PREVIOUS PAGE: *In this classic fairy tale of love, a beautiful princess is cursed by an evil fairy. Upon pricking her finger on a spinning wheel she falls into a profound sleep for one hundred years. The curse can only be broken by her being kissed by a prince. As the years pass the castle becomes over-run with ivy. However, one day a passing prince spies the castle and upon entering sees the beautiful princess, kisses her and she awakes.*

I made a garland for her head, And bracelets too, and fragrant zone; She look'd at me as she did love, And made sweet moan.

LA BELLE DAME SANS MERCI, JOHN KEATS

ABOVE: *This painting by Sir Frank Dicksee, entitled* **La Belle Dame Sans Merci** *was almost certainly inspired by the Keats poem of the same name. The image of the 'knight in shining armour' is a common one and Jungian analysis suggests that when a man experiences such a dream, he has awakened the female aspect of his sleeping psyche.*

Freud on love

Freud believed that a dream develops directly from some aspect of the unconscious mind. He proposed that dreams of love and sex, like all dreams, actually function on two levels. They have a manifest content—what they seem to mean—and a latent content—what they actually mean. Using free association to discover the connections his patients made between symbols, Freud aimed to reveal a dream's latent content in order to arrive at a true interpretation of a love dream. A classic example of latent and manifest dream content is the symbol of the house whose basement, downstairs, upstairs, attic, and front porch are often identified as anatomical symbols or body parts.

Freud and his followers would propose that dream symbols are necessary for deeply repressed wishes to escape censorship. Freud had a large influence on "standard" interpretations for commonly occurring sexual symbols. For example, towers, pencils, pistons, and other items which share functional, physical, or linguistic similarities are thought to be phallic symbols. Similarly boxes, caves, doorways, and tunnels are seen to represent the vagina.

Rachel's dream

A young woman named Rachel had just met a new colleague at work and found him very attractive sexually. Yet that night she did not dream of handsome Dave, but dreamt of the spire at Westminster Cathedral. When she woke up she realized

LEFT: Freud with his wife, Martha Bernays. Married in 1886, they had six children.

that Dave had told her that he lives in the London borough of Westminster, and the phallic symbolism of the spire was quite obvious. It is worth looking for this kind of symbolism in our dreams as our initial attraction to another is often sexual in its nature. A dream of making love is most likely to be a case of wish fulfilment or wishful thinking rather than anything prophetic. Bearing all of this in mind, it is not helpful to generalize about all such dream symbols, and reputable dream analysis should always be sensitive to the dreamer's own life and emotional processes. As you read the directory section of the book it is worth holding onto this idea.

The connections between love and the erotic become inescapable in Freud's work. Freud's heavy emphasis on sexuality as the source of all psychological disorders implied that the sexual interpretation of dreams was the single key to unlock their meanings. Freud proposed that a skilled analyst could use dream interpretation to reveal the unconscious needs and wishes of the dreamer and prevent them from continuing to be fixated or stuck at a particular phase of their development. Freud, who described dreams as the "royal road to the unconscious," believed that repression and other protective defense mechanisms operate less completely during sleep. Thus a patient's dreams, correctly interpreted, can help unconscious conflicts to be resolved to some extent.

The secret love of Sigmund Freud

Freud talked and wrote on issues of relationships and sexuality in great depth. For many years, however, there has been much speculation about Freud's own love life. It has been suggested that Freud and his sister-in-law Minna Bernays were lovers. Some go so far as to say that Minna even conceived Freud's child but underwent an abortion. Carl Jung is said to have known about this when Minna, in a state of distress, confided in Jung. Freudian scholars however, remain divided about the nature of their relationship. Some say that it is merely fact-based fiction that exaggerates a close working relationship.

Jung on love

Jung saw the world of dreams and love quite differently from Freud. He rejected Freud's heavy emphasis on sexuality as the key to all psychic disorders. For Jung dreams were not only a way of understanding what was wrong in the psyche—for example if we are a repeated victim, if we are addicted to sex or can never find love. He valued dreams for their ability to help the dreamer solve these problems. So in Jung's view dream analysis is not just concerned with correcting that which is wrong about us, rather it is about the creative unfolding and development of our whole potential. Some Jungian analysts may even go so far as to say that one can achieve closeness to another through the use of a dream. A relationship could therefore be improved by encouraging it to flourish within one's dream.

In 1903 Jung married Emma Rauschenbach, having fallen in love with her six years previously. He apparently caught a glimpse of the young girl when she was just fourteen at the top of a staircase and immediately thought to himself that "this will be the girl that I marry." A Jungian would describe this as a classic case of anima projection since Jung knew nothing about the girl, but was nevertheless sure that he knew and liked what he thought he knew. Between the years of 1904 and 1914 Emma gave birth to five children—four boys and a girl.

Jung's love

I saw her in a dream which was like a vision. She stood at some distance from me, looking at me squarely. She was in her prime, perhaps about thirty, and wearing the dress which had been made for her many years before by my cousin the medium. It was perhaps the most beautiful thing she had ever worn. Her expression was neither joyful nor sad, but, rather, **objectively wise and understanding, without the slightest emotional reaction, as though she were beyond the mist of affects. I knew it was not she but a portrait she had made or commissioned for me. It contained the beginning of our relationship, the events of fifty-three years of marriage, and the end of her life also. Face to face with such wholeness one remains speechless, for it can scarcely be comprehended.**

C.G. Jung, *Memories, Dreams, Reflections*, 1963.

Dream love exercise

Visualize your partner as vividly as possible just before you drop off to sleep. Practice over a series of nights if you do not have success initially. Your dreams may depict a relationship that is parallel to your waking one or it may throw up all sorts of symbols and dilemmas that call for interpretation and discussion. Try to make some time to discuss these dream symbols with your partner and it may enhance the understanding and develop the closeness between you.

Jung developed a concept called the "soul image" in relation to our human need to create a sense of wholeness. This tends to be an archetypal image. Jung coined the term

READY !

"anima" to represent the feminine aspect of the male psyche, which in modern Western society is often repressed. For a woman the "animus" represents the more traditionally masculine traits within the female psyche. Jungian analysts argue that every man has a female component and every woman has a male component and that if this aspect of the psyche is suppressed, then it can lead to dire consequences. In the Western world it has been considered a virtue to do the manly thing and for men to repress their emotions and their femininity. Until recently women were socially prohibited from displaying any signs of masculinity. This may be because of man's fear of the feminine and therefore of women, leading men to suppress women and keep them subordinate. A further consequence of the suppression of femininity in a world dominated by men is war. Many Jungians suggest that war is a consequence

of men's aggressiveness which has not been balanced by love and patience to achieve harmony.

In dreams, the symbols that represent the soul image appear as the opposite sex. Thus a man's anima may be represented by his sister; a woman's animus by her brother. Symbols of the animus that can appear in our dreams are a bull, lion, phallus (erect penis) or any of the other phallic symbols described earlier. The eagle is generally seen as male as it is associated with high altitudes and sky. The earth and related symbols, however, are seen as female (Mother Earth), and tell the dreamer of sensuousness and sexual femininity. Other dream symbols that represent the anima would be the cat, a tiger, a cave, a ship or any other vessel. The sea is seen as feminine, as it is associated with the waters of the womb. Caves are hollow and womb-like. If you fail to acknowledge and become acquainted with your soul image, Jungians argue, you are likely to project it onto members of the opposite sex and this can lead to disastrous relationships. A sensitive woman, for example, may be attracted to uncaring detached partners. Jung felt that dreams can be used to explore our soul images to help us to become a fuller and more balanced person.

The archetypal figures of the
love hero and damsel in distress
are abundant across cultures
and folklore and permeate our
dream worlds.

LEFT: *Jung's theories were often inspired by myth and legend, such as that of* **Cupid** *and* **Psyche**. *Francois Picot's painting shows Cupid visiting his lover, Psyche, at night—the only time when he was allowed to see her as she was not permitted to look at his face. Psyche was a beautiful princess of whom the goddess Venus, Cupid's mother, became jealous. Cupid and Psyche fell in love after Cupid mistakenly shot them both with his arrows. Despite Venus's jealousy and the difficult tasks she sets for Psyche, the pair eventually married.*

Myths and legends

It is said that a dream expresses the unconscious dynamics within an individual, whereas a myth can express the dynamics of the collective mind of a society. Therefore through myth the unconscious mind can send its concerns to the conscious mind. By learning the symbolic language of dreams and myths the dreamer can develop an understanding of their inner psyche and learn to respond to its current needs.

My Lords, if you would hear a high tale of love and death, here is that of Tristan and Queen Iseult; how to their full joy but to their sorrow also, they loved each other, and how at last, they died of that love together upon one day; she by him and he by her.
Tristan and Iseult

It is argued that the story of Tristan and Iseult is one of the great stories of all time. Such a myth does more than lift us or provide good entertainment. If we learn to listen to myths, legends, and our personal dreams we can slowly develop a deeper psychological understanding and greater knowledge of our own psyche. Jung was one of the first to draw on the rich tapestry of stories from across the world and throughout history to formulate his ideas on dream analysis and archetypal figures. Such dream characters often prevail in dreams concerned with matters of the heart.

The dream image of the love hero or knight in shining armor who rescues his partner in the face of adversity is a particularly common one. Jungian analysts have suggested that when a man experiences a dream featuring the mythical rescue he has unlocked his femininity or anima and awakened the female aspect of his sleeping psyche. Without dreams, these theorists suggest such an emotional awakening would be impossible. The archetypal figures of the love hero and damsel in distress are abundant across cultures and folklore and permeate our dream worlds. The Greek hero Perseus saves the Ethiopian Princess Andromeda from a sea monster and later marries her. In a Western European folktale variant Sleeping Beauty is woken and saved from the sleep of death by a prince. In the fairy tale all the other courtiers who have also been asleep for a hundred years awake. Jungian theorists suggest that the kiss of life refers to the unleashing of the anima.

This notion of dream love continues in contemporary times. In Tolstoy's novel *Anna Karenina* where Anna has betrayed her marriage to Alexy Alexandrovich Karenin because of her passion for Vronsky, Tolstoy writes:

In her dreams, when she had no control over her thoughts, her position appeared to her in all its shocking nakedness. One dream she had almost every night. She dreamt that both at once were her husbands and lavished kisses on her… but this dream weighed on her like a nightmare, and she woke from it filled with horror.

Oedipus myth and complex

Freud, like Jung, also used ancient stories in developing theories about love, attachment and the nature of relationships. The Oedipus complex is one of Freud's best-known theories and, perhaps, his most influential. The term essentially refers to a group of largely unconscious ideas and feelings centering on the wish to possess the parent of the opposite sex and eliminate that of the same sex. The complex is said to emerge in the young male child between the age of three to seven years, when he desires his mother and consequently feels envy and rage against his father.

The complex is named after the hero of two tragedies by the Greek playwright Sophocles, about the mythical Oedipus who killed his father, and then fell in love with and married his mother without knowing that they were his parents. In the story, the Oracle predicts that the innocent prince of Thebes will murder his father and marry his mother. His father, hoping to avoid this fate, abandons his child on a hillside, with his feet pierced, to die of starvation and exposure. But some strangers find the helpless child and raise him to the best of their ability. Unknowingly he returns to fulfil the prophecy. He slays the king and frees the kingdom from the oppression of a wild and evil creature—the Theban Sphinx. He takes the queen, who is in fact his mother, in marriage and then realizes what he has done. He feels horrible and full of remorse for this crime, though actually he is not personally responsible for it, and gouges out his own eyes and once again wanders blind and exiled.

Although the term Oedipus complex can now be applied to both males and females, at first Oedipus referred only to the male version of the complex and in the young female child the Electra complex was said to exist, derived from another tragedy by Sophocles. Electra's story is not quite an accurate counterpart, however, since Electra, rather than directly murdering her mother, asked her brother to do it on her behalf to avenge her father's death. Girls, like boys, fear their impulses and fear that their wishes will cause their mother to stop loving them or to hurt them. Thus they must repress their desires and learn to identify with their mother.

According to Freud this complex is a universal phenomenon no matter what culture you are from. He claimed that it was responsible for much unconscious guilt. Many of our dreams focus on the death of a parent and their power can be frightening. However, feelings of love are not straightforward and can be found on the other side of the coin as hate. It is vital that such dreams be interpreted with caution. It is important to make connections with waking associations around the dream and to determine whether there may be issues of wish fulfilment, envy, and intense love or passion that are being brought to consciousness through the unconscious world of your dreams.

Is the person in the dream really the object of our intense feelings of love or is there another way to read the dream?

Laboratory love

Rather than drawing on the individual case study, like Freud and Jung, experimental psychologists have made attempts to be more rigorously scientific in their investigations into the concepts of love and dreams. In dream analysis much emphasis is placed on the intensity of symbols in an attempt to discover whether the dreamer is in the realm of loving or liking someone or something. Z. Rubin in the mid-1970s developed a scale to evaluate key components of love and he attempted to use the scale to differentiate between the notions of loving and liking. Rubin argued that loving, as opposed to liking, consists of three key elements: attachment (powerful desire to be in the presence of another), caring (the willingness to sacrifice for the sake of another), and intimacy (the union or bond between two individuals). Therefore dreams of separation and goodbyes can be connected to Rubin's notion of attachment and may be a signal for the dreamer to notice their feelings of love for someone nearby. Dreams of children, of vulnerable animals, of tending to the sick or elderly are likely to be connected to what Rubin described as caring. If feelings of intensity and intimacy accompany these dream symbols then the message to the dreamer is likely to be one of love and should be listened to.

Some bold researchers have tried to study the concept of love within a controlled scientific laboratory. Such researchers, often social psychologists, claim that romantic love or perhaps sexual attraction can be replicated in laboratory conditions. Following a wealth of experiments encouraging subjects to look at sexual scenarios while measuring physiological responses, researchers have concluded that the most important ingredients in producing an emotional experience like love are a state of physical arousal (beating heart, sweating, shallow breathing) combined with an emotional explanation of why that arousal has occurred. This has important implications that can assist us in the process of dream analysis. If we wake from a dream that involves someone whom we are in a close relationship with or perhaps long to be with, it is important to check on our physical state. Are we aroused by our dream images? If so, to what do we attribute these physical sensations? Are there any other messages that our body could be telling us through these sensations? Is the person in the dream really the object of our intense feelings of love or is there another way to read the dream, for example as in the case of Claire (overleaf)?

Claire was a forty-year-old woman who was going through a difficult period in her marriage. Over the past two months, Claire had recently begun to have recurring dreams about her ex-husband. On waking she was highly aroused, her heart was beating, she was breathing quickly, and she was covered in a cold sweat. Her ex-husband always appeared in her dreams as an ideal partner—both sexually and intellectually. Most nights they talked intimately and engaged in passionate dream sex. On waking, Claire was shocked by her feelings and was unsure about how to interpret the messages that were held within these dreams. Initially Claire made a very concrete interpretation and believed that she had actually married the wrong man. She was so panicked that she had decided to contact her ex-lover. Claire started to talk to her husband and others about the meaning of the dream and then realized that by constructing an illusion of an ideal past with her ex-husband, Claire was actually trying to avoid the difficulties of her present life and her marriage. Once she had acknowledged this, Claire felt liberated and was free to address her current life situation and her relationship with her new husband. If we can hold onto the thoughts and sensations that inhabit our dreams of love, then we may be able to harness their potential and use them to improve and develop in our waking lives.

CLAIRE'S CASE

Narcissism—self-love

It is not love we should have painted as blind, but self love.
Voltaire.

The term narcissism originates from the Greek myth which tells of the death of the young man Narcissus, who was so enraptured by the beauty of his own reflection in a pool that he pined away longing to possess his own image. His name has now become synonymous with extreme self-love or over-involvement with the self. There are a range of theories that contribute to an understanding of an extreme narcissistic personality, but they all tend to agree that this disorder develops in early childhood. They suggest that when parents interact with their children in an unloving manner this can cause the children to feel unworthy. They can feel rejected. In order to help themselves, such children can defend against these uncomfortable feelings by telling themselves that they are actually perfect and desirable. Other theorists, mainly behavioral ones, contradict this hypothesis and propose that it those children who get excessive amounts of praise and positive feedback who go on to develop narcissistic personalities in later life.

Dreams can be used to explore a person's beliefs about themselves and can be used to break down notions of grandiosity. In dream scenarios where the appearance of kings, queens, beautiful people or celebrities are rife, it is worth noticing your relationship to these characters. Were they aspects of your grandiose self? Were you or others able to reach them or were these characters so self-centered that they were unreachable? This line of questioning could provide you with a valuable insight into your own narcissistic tendencies.

ABOVE: *John William Waterhouse's painting,* Echo and Narcissus, *depicts the Greek myth of Narcissus, who was so in love with own reflection he ignored the advances of girls and beautiful nymphs like Echo, pictured here.*

CHAPTER 9

Sex

The tragedy is when you've got sex in the head instead of down where it belongs.

SEXUAL OR EROTIC DREAMS ARE GENERALLY CONSIDERED TO BE EXPRESSIONS OF WISH FULFILMENT, OR A MEANS OF RELEASING SEXUAL TENSION. IN THE 1800S SEXUAL DREAMS WERE CONSIDERED TO BE A GREAT SOURCE OF WORRY TO THE MEN AND WOMEN WHO HAD THEM BECAUSE AT THAT TIME SEXUAL DREAMS WERE THOUGHT TO CAUSE MENTAL AND PHYSICAL ILLNESS. HOWEVER, IT WOULD BE OVERSIMPLISTIC TO DESCRIBE ALL SEXUAL DREAMS AS A FORM OF FRUSTRATION OR FULFILMENT.

Dreams of nudity

Dreams of appearing naked in public are extremely common and generally tell of some underlying fear of exposure. Such dreams are rarely connected to feelings about sex, and if anything are probably linked to experiences of embarrassment, rebellion, or even a lack of caring. If you dream of nudity, the main thing to ask yourself is how you experienced that state in the dream. Were you deeply ashamed or did you enjoy celebrating the freedom of being without clothes? Other dreams of nakedness can be connected to ideas about truth and honesty.

Andrew's dream
Andrew recently woke up from a dream where he was watching his favorite sports team playing. He was in the stands watching with all his friends and family. He saw his mom and dad nearby, his brothers and their children, his friends, and some colleagues from work. They were all dressed in warm clothes. Andrew had nothing on at all. However, in the dream and on waking he did not feel embarrassed about being naked. He felt at ease with his favorite people around him and his favorite team playing. For Andrew this dream seemed to represent a total state of contentment that he was feeling.

Many sexual dreams are disturbing, particularly if they involve violence or perversion. If persistently disturbing sexual dreams trouble you, it may be worth seeking professional guidance. If in a dream you find yourself enjoying something that is the opposite of your usual sexual preferences, it may be worthwhile to explore this further. After all, our dreams do come from deep within us, so perhaps the unconscious is trying to communicate something, such as an appeal for a greater degree of understanding in the realm of sex and sexuality.

In Shakespeare's *Othello*, Cassio has a vivid erotic dream about Desdemona, which is witnessed by Iago. Relaying the tale, Iago defends Cassio, but Othello is unconvinced. This passage marks the significance of the dream in Elizabethan times:

OTHELLO:	*O monstrous! monstrous!*
IAGO:	*Nay, this was but his dream.*
OTHELLO:	*But this denoted a foregone conclusion.*
IAGO:	*'Tis a shrewd doubt, though it be but a dream.*

William Shakespeare, *Othello*, c. 1600

PREVIOUS PAGE: *Paulo Fiammingo's* **Lovers.**

RIGHT: *Hieronymous Bosch's triptych* **The Garden of Earthly Desires** *depicts man's progress through sin. Some believe that he may have painted this work about the beliefs of a heretical sect, called the Adamites—from the nakedness of Adam—which believed in nudism and free sexual relations.*

Freud used the term sexuality in a very broad way to mean that which is sensuous or the desire for sensuous pleasure.

Freud on sex

Freud developed the famous and often ridiculed theory of infantile sexuality. Whatever you may think of the theory, it does greatly affect current understandings of sexual symbolism in dreams. Freud believed that adult sexuality—that is the way in which sexual organs are aroused, often but not always involving an act of penetration—developed from sexuality that was already present in childhood. Freud used the term sexuality in a very broad way to mean that which is sensuous or the desire for sensuous pleasure. In a newborn baby sensuous pleasure is said to be felt throughout the body on the surface of the skin as well as internally. Later it is said to become focused on particular parts of the body such as the mouth, anus and the genitals.

The oral stage is the earliest developmental phase and encompasses approximately the first eighteen months of life. Oral pleasure is said to occur when the infant sucks at the mother's breast—the source of nourishment and pleasure. Such pleasure may be found in biting and sucking other objects too. Freud considered these to be mere substitutes for the nipple. At the beginning of the oral stage the child is said to be highly narcissistic, solely focusing on his or her own needs, with no recognition of the outside world. Over time, however, the child begins to perceive the mother and others as separate objects rather than extensions of himself.

The anal stage occurs, according to Freud and his followers, in the second eighteen months of life. Freud said that anal pleasure is experienced in the withholding or passing of feces and the child becomes very interested in his bodily functions.

The child passes through the phallic stage at roughly three or four years of age. Freud said that genital pleasure occurs from touching or playing with the penis or the vagina. At this stage boys apparently become attracted to their mother as a fully separate sexual object (the Oedipus complex) and girls to their father (the Electra complex) (discussed in Chapter 8 on Love). It is important that girls and boys resolve these conflicts by coming to identify with the parent of their own sex.

The latency stage occurs from about six years of age and lasts until a child is about twelve years old. A child's sexual desires are said to temporarily go dormant and their libidinal energy is invested in developing new skills and interests. During this stage children tend to seek same-sex friends and to dislike people from the opposite sex.

The child's sexual urges reemerge once again with the onset of puberty, the "genital stage." Sexual relationships begin to develop, although in the early stages adolescents still hold many narcissistic qualities.

How does this relate to our understanding of dreams?

It is thought that not all of us actually make a trouble-free transition through all of these developmental stages, and therefore do not actually achieve "normal" adult sexuality. Many of us have hang-ups of one kind or another and according to Freud we get stuck or fixated in one or another stage of infantile sexual development.

Freud believed that we can easily spot where a person has become fixated, or has become stuck, because their behavior patterns have certain give-away characteristics. Fixation at the oral or sucking phase, he says, shows itself in people who overeat, suck their thumb or bite their nails. These indicate a dependant personality who has not yet become completely separate from their mother figure. They have not yet learnt to stand on their own two feet. This fixation can also show an aggressive type who lashes out at people.

Untidy, wasteful, and extravagant people, on the other hand, are thought to be stuck in the anal phase, where pleasure is said to be found in expelling feces. Where pleasure is gained in retaining feces, you will find a neat, compulsively fastidious person.

Fixation at the pre-adult genital stage of development may show itself in either exhibitionism or auto-eroticism.

Our dreams therefore can tell us where we are in this process of development and an understanding of Freud's theory may provide you with a valuable guide to understanding your dreams.

Gary's dream

Gary dreamt that he was speeding along a dangerous cliff-side road in his brand new red MG sports car. He was taking hairpin bends at high speed without worry. His girlfriend, who was sitting in the back seat, was scared and begged him to slow down. Gary ignored her wishes and carried on speeding despite her fear. He started to skid and was beginning to lose control and began careering over the edge when he woke up in a cold sweat.

A sports car is an obvious and well-known phallic symbol in many ways. It is high-speed and powerful, with the man seen to be in the driving seat. In the car he is penetrating the environment around him.

In this dream Gary seems to be going too fast for his girlfriend, who interestingly is seated behind him. This seems to be a warning for Gary to slow down in their relationship. Gary is sexually confident and his new girlfriend is much less so. It seems that he needs to take his time in developing a trusting sexual relationship or this relationship could come crashing down around him.

Penis envy

Penis envy is said to be the primary yearning that a girl is thought to have for a penis during her phallic phase of development. It has become one of the most controversial concepts in Freudian theory. He claimed that penis envy lies at the basis of women's feelings of inferiority because the young female sees herself as an incomplete male. He believed that a young girl may react to this imagined castration in many ways.

For example, she might avoid clitoral sex. Seeing her clitoris as an inferior penis makes her lose interest in it. She might become a lesbian. She might become career minded and become a man's equal. She might avoid sex altogether to avoid her feelings of inferiority. She may fail to resolve the Oedipal stage and all men in her adult life will take on the role of father substitutes. Or she may resolve this phase and will be satisfied by taking possession of a man's penis in a heterosexual relationship.

Lolita

In Vladimir Nabakov's novel *Lolita* we can see the Oedipal complex functioning. Humbert Humbert is lodging with Charlotte Haze and her young daughter Lolita. In the story he wakes from a night's sleep and turns the light on to note down a dream. That night at dinner Mrs Haze had said that she and her daughter would venture on a picnic the next day with Humbert.

As I lay in bed, erotically musing before trying to go to sleep, I thought of a final scheme how to profit by the picnic to come. I was aware that mother Haze hated my darling for being so sweet on me. So I planned my lake day with a view to satisfying the mother. To her alone I would talk; but at some appropriate moment I would say I had left my wrist watch or my sunglasses in that glade yonder—and plunge with my nymphet into the wood. Reality at this juncture withdrew, and the Quest for the Glasses turned into a quiet little orgy with a singularly knowing, cheerful, corrupt and compliant Lolita behaving as reason knew she could not possibly behave. At 3 a.m. I swallowed a sleeping pill, and presently, a dream that was not a sequel but a parody revealed to me, with a kind of meaningful clarity, the lake I had never yet visited: it was glazed over with a sheet of emerald ice, and a pockmarked Eskimo was trying in vain to break it with a pickaxe, although imported mimosas and oleanders flowered on its gravely banks. I am sure Dr. Blanche Schwarzmann would have paid me a sack of shillings for adding such a libidream to her files. Unfortunately, the rest of it was frankly eclectic. Big Haze and little Haze rode on horseback around the lake, and I rode too, dutifully bobbing up and down, bowlegs astraddle although there was no horse between them, only elastic air— one of those little omissions due to the absent-mindedness of the dream agent.

Vladimir Nabakov, Lolita, 1955.

Dali's 'The Great Masturbator'

The title of Salvador Dali's painting *The Great Masturbator* also makes explicit the subject of his other painting, *The Lugubrious Game*. Dali himself described The Great Masturbator as "the expression of my heterosexual anxiety." In 1929, when this picture was painted, the Spanish painter Dali was still a virgin. He was allegedly inhibited by deep-rooted fears of female sexuality and anal obsessions. It is said that these anxieties never left him, although he did have a sexu-

al relationship with Gala Eluard. She left her poet husband Paul Eluard for Dali and later married him. *The Great Masturbator* was painted after their relationship had begun. It was inspired by a nineteenth-century picture of a woman smelling an arum lilly. Dali replaced the lily with a male figure. The woman and male figure emerge from the Dali head which had already appeared in *The Lugubrious Game*.

Dali acknowledged masturbation as his only means to orgasm, but was never prepared to concede that this was a tragedy. However, he became the only painter in history to make masturbation a major theme of his work.

I took too much wine. Dreamed of walk with Joan and Connie... Then of showing Joanna a beautiful snake, which I told her was an innocent one

Sexual dream symbols

Symbols of male and female genitalia abound in our waking environments and they can easily enter our dream worlds at an unconscious level. Some of these images may represent certain unconscious sexual expression or desires, while others may not, but it may be worth looking out for.

■ A cigar or cigarette may symbolize a penis. Freud admitted that his avid cigar smoking was possibly a substitute for masturbation.

■ A car may represent the penis—especially if it is powerfully driven with a strong thrusting motor.

■ A cave may represent the womb or a place of conception or birth, as would a cupboard or empty vessel.

■ Flowers, lilies, figs, and ripening fruits all have female sexual symbolism.

■ Spires and towers standing high and erect are often thought to represent the penis. A weathercock on the tower may be a particularly strong sexual symbol, especially in a woman's dream.

■ Horses, especially a stallion, may be a symbol of sexuality and mounting a horse may be a representation of a sexual act.

■ Darts, fingers, snakes, guns, hammers, screwdrivers, horns of an animal, icicles, javelins and spears, lorries and engines, obelisks, and poles are all phallic symbols.

In John Ruskin's diaries (1868) the phallic symbolism of the snake was clear in one of his dreams:

I took too much wine. Dreamed of walk with Joan and Connie... Then of showing Joanna a beautiful snake, which I told her was an innocent one; it had a slender neck and a green ring around it, and I made her feel its scales. Then she made me feel it and it became a fat thing, like a leech and adhered to my hand, so that I could hardly pull it off—and so I woke.

RIGHT: *As with dreams, certain images in painting hold sexual connotations. Many painters used symbolism to represent sexual content. Picking fruit from trees was seen as having sexual intercourse as the fruit itself represents sexual organs. In dreams too flowers, lilies, figs and ripening fruits all have female sexual symbolism.*

LEFT: *This painting shows the goddess Chinnamasta (meaning desire) as she cuts off her head and distributes her life-energy into the universe, thus bestowing upon her worshippers, shown in this painting to be a man and a woman having sex, whatever they ask for and desire.*

Jung on sex

Jung differed from Freud in areas of sexual theory and libido. In 1911 and 1912 he published a book in two parts titled *Metamorphoses and Symbols of the Libido*. In English it was published with the title *The Psychology of the Unconscious*. It consisted of Jung's reflections on a series of fantasies recorded by an American woman who went under the name Miss Miller. Jung rejected Freud's idea of the libido being exclusively sexual. Instead Jung suggested that the libido was a non-specific energy and that sexuality was but one form that this energy might take. He also rejected the Oedipus and Electra complex. He acknowledged that small boys and girls could become highly attached and attracted to the parent of the opposite sex, but he disputed the fact that this attachment or conflict was sexual. Jung regarded the mother as a nourishing, protective figure rather than an object of incestuous desire. So to Jung the son's

longing for his mother was a spiritual quest and rebirth rather than a sexual yearning.

Jung also developed the concepts of the anima and animus discussed in Chapter 8 on Love. For Jung, soul-less sex can be thought of as another consequence of man's repressed anima. In contrast, soulful sex can aid in achieving the perfect balance or harmony or wholeness within oneself. This has been recognized in many Eastern traditions, such as the Tantric mystic–meditative traditions of Hinduism and Buddhism, and is being more widely recognized in parts of the West. It is thought that sex can only reach those levels of balance and pure harmony where there is worship—that is when each partner in the sexual relationship acknowledges the value and treasures within their sexual opposite. The aggressive and repressed male may reduce sex to a purely physical act where his partner is objectified. The repressed woman may do the same or may become completely disinterested in sexual relations because of fear. Jungians believe therefore that it is essential to integrate our anima and animus for individual and social progress. They believe that your soul image leads your conscious ego safely into the unconscious and out again.

Theseus and the minotaur

In Greek myth, Theseus needed to penetrate the labyrinth in Crete in order to slay the monstrous Minotaur. The beautiful maiden Ariadne used her thread to help him to go into the labyrinth and find his way out again. If we use Jungian thinking to understand this myth, the labyrinth is a symbol of the unconscious. The Minotaur is the frightening monster that represents repressed material that we are afraid of and would rather not deal with. It has been neglected and gone wild. The slaying of the monster represents the facing and taming of the dangerous matter and bringing it under our control. But the slaying can only be achieved by love and by acknowledging what has been neglected. The soul image (Ariadne) reconciles the unconscious and the conscious.

Anima/animus visualization task

Sit down and consider what aspects of your personality are most like those of the opposite sex. If you are female they might be aggression, competitiveness, machismo, or anything else. If you are male they might be sensitivity, emotionality, passivity, and so on. Then try to imagine a person of the opposite sex who has only these one-sided traits. What are they like? What do they look like? How do you interact with them? Do you like them? How do they hold themselves? What do they talk about? Would you want to be friendly with this person in real life? Look out for the opposite characteristics that are missing from your own psyche and bring them into your awareness when you can.

RELATIONS BETWEEN FREUD AND JUNG

Apparently, neither Freud nor Jung were easy men to get along with. Freud tended to fall out with friends. He fell out not only with Jung and Adler, but also with other colleagues such as Breuer, Fliess, and Meynert. Jung apparently had considerable difficulty relating to men and had few male friends except for one childhood companion. Jung was said to be much more comfortable in the company of women. Women were said to be powerfully attracted to him and gathered round him to form a sizeable following, which became known in Zurich as the *Jungfrauen*. Jung grew impatient with Freud's dogmatism and Freud seemed to be edgy about his authority and credibility. In old age Jung still vividly recalled how Freud had said to him, "My dear Jung, promise me never to abandon the sexual theory. That is the most essential thing of all. You see we must make a dogma of it, an unshakable bulwark" (Anthony Stevens, *On Jung*, 1999).

Their differences in character and beliefs seem likely to have emerged from their own backgrounds. Freud came from an urban Jewish background and an education that led him into empirical science. Freud's mother was apparently a beautiful woman who doted on him, giving him much love and attention. Jung was a rural Protestant, whose young mind was taken up with ideas of romantic idealism. His mother was plain and prone to bouts of depression, which caused her to spend time away in hospital when Jung was young. Freud's relationship with his own mother and his own childhood experience moved him to develop ideas about Oedipus. Jung's period of maternal absence and his religious background led him to turn inward to seek spiritual security within himself.

CHAPTER 10

Change

Change is the Law of Life. And those who look only to the past or the present are certain to miss the future.

THE EXPERIENCE OF CHANGE IS A FUNDAMENTAL PHYSICAL AND PSYCHOLOGICAL PROCESS THAT WE ENCOUNTER AS HUMAN BEINGS IN ALL ASPECTS OF OUR LIVES. AS WE GROW OLDER, EACH BIRTHDAY, NEW YEAR CELEBRATION, AND FRESH SEASON OFFERS A NEW OPPORTUNITY TO MANAGE CHANGE. WHETHER IT IS A MUNDANE CHANGE OF TAKING A DIFFERENT ROUTE TO WORK, OR A SUBSTANTIAL CHANGE LIKE GIVING BIRTH, ALL CHANGE INVOLVES BOTH LOSSES AND GAINS. DREAMS THAT ARE CENTERED ON CHANGE ARE ABUNDANT BECAUSE CHANGE IS PRESENT IN MOST ASPECTS OF OUR WAKING LIVES. DREAMS ABOUT CHANGE SHOULD BE CLOSELY LISTENED TO. THEY CAN BE USED AS A WAY OF HARNESSING ENERGY, EXPRESSING AMBIVALENCE ABOUT AN EVENT, OR EVEN PROCESSING THE THOUGHTS AND FEELINGS THAT SURROUND THAT CHANGE.

Dreams of a new job, moving house, and new relationships are all symbolic of aspects of life change and the dreamer will need to brainstorm around the contents of such dreams to try to understand their meaning in depth. Dreams of birth, gardens, vegetation, and anything to do with fertility are often associated with positive change and new beginnings for the dreamer. Any dream of a rites of passage ceremony, such as a wedding, funeral, or birthday all contain change symbolism and should be studied carefully. It is important to notice the feelings that surrounded the experiences in the dream. How did others react to the dream change event? Was there happiness or sadness in the air or were there too many obstacles in the dream that prevented the occurrence of the event? Given the number of changes that we experience in our lives and the number of losses and gains that are contained within, it is not surprising that so much dream imagery is associated with change.

Dreams of death, of saying goodbye or farewell to friends or family also indicate times of change. Such dreams do not necessarily mean that you are going to say goodbye to those people, rather that you may be ending a particular phase of your life. The dreamer should be able to find clues as to what aspect of life is being left behind. If the dead person in the dream is the dreamer, then this suggests that some aspect of the dreamer's personality or inner self needs to be left behind, or perhaps some issue needs to be let go. If a parent has died

in the dream it may mean that it is time for the dreamer to let go of parental ties or cut the umbilical cord.

… this change is at once the death of that which was before.
Lucretius, *On the Nature of Things,* 1st century B.C.

Keith's dream
Keith had just turned forty and celebrated with a big house party involving all his favorite friends and family. He had a great time, but that night had an interesting dream. Keith could not remember all the details of the dream, but the most striking part of it was that his teenage hero, singer–songwriter Bob Dylan, had died in the dream. As a teenager Keith had adored the lyrics and music of Bob Dylan. He had bought every record and seen him in concert on many occasions. The words and music of Bob Dylan had accompanied Keith through all the hard times of his youth and he sought comfort in them when

things were tough. However, during the dream and on waking, Keith did not feel any sense of loss at the death. He was quite surprised and confused at this reaction. He felt no sadness at all and in fact felt some element of freedom and relief that he couldn't initially explain. On further exploration Keith realized that the death of dream Bob had been cathartic in some way and symbolized the release that he had felt at growing older and leaving his troubled past behind him. Perhaps the birthday had triggered the dream, as Keith was now "officially middle-aged." In some respects bidding farewell to the teenage hero was more of a gain than a loss for Keith, as he was able to let go of the past and say hello to the new phase of his life.

Dreams of people in disguise can often be an indication of processes of change. It is important to notice who was disguised in the dream and what they were disguised as. If they were disguised as something frightening, this may be a clue to the dreamer's fears about everyday life. If the disguise was joyous, it may represent an element of wish fulfilment for the dreamer.

Dreams of radical change, such as revolution, war, fighting, or even a radical house make-over, may suggest that the dreamer is experiencing a degree of inner conflict and that some aspect of life needs a radical overhaul. It is important to listen to such dreams and where possible to act on them.

The issue of change and dreams has been portrayed in art and culture throughout time and is perhaps a fundamental component of dream work. "When Gregor Samsa woke up one morning from unsettling dreams, he found himself changed in his bed into a monstrous vermin." Franz Kafka used this notion of dream and change

PREVIOUS PAGE: *Surrealist artists like Salvador Dali often used images of change and dreams to inform their work, as in this piece the* **Metamorphosis of Narcissus**, *based on the ancient myth of Narcissus who fell in love with his own reflection.*

ABOVE: *Dreams of people in disguises, such as in this illustration of a Greek actor with masks, indicate processes of change.*

in his classic text, *Metamorphosis*. The Surrealist artists, particularly Salvador Dali, used experiences of change and dream change to inform their work. This is well illustrated in Dali's *Metamorphosis of Narcissus* based on the ancient myth of Narcissus who fell in love with his own reflection.

Adaptation

Jung grounded his theory of archetypes and the collective unconscious in biological thinking. For according to Jung, the psychic life of the individual must be seen in the context of the entire species: "every individual life is the same as the eternal life of the species" (C.G. Jung, *Collected Works* 11, para.146).

Jung suggested that adaptation was necessary for all species to survive their environment. Young creatures of all species, including humankind, begin life with the innate, inbuilt tools that are necessary to enable them to go through the process of adaptation. Continual adaptation carries on for the life span of each individual in the context of their environment, or what Jung called *Umwelt*. Learning, said Jung, plays a vital role in the adaptation process.

If we relate this idea to the human species then we can see that a human infant in Jung's view is clearly not a blank slate on which adults and other aspects of the environment imprint their markings. Jung would suggest that a human infant is a complex being with a range of inbuilt responses and behaviors and expectations that emerge in the right environment. The archetypal equipment of a newborn enables it to adapt to its situation, just as our ancestors did millions of years ago. Jung suggested that other psychic structures such as the self, the ego, the persona, the shadow, and the anima or animus all perform adaptive functions on the psyche.

THE SELF

According to Jung the self is the greatest psychic organ of adaptation. It is, he argues, the organizing force behind the whole personality. The self is responsible for bringing about the best by adjustment to each life-cycle situation. The self has its own function of seeking its own fulfilment from life. The goal of the self is wholeness. Jung called this lifelong search for wholeness "individuation." The self, although rooted in biology, is said to hold the mysteries of the soul. The self provides the means of adaptation not only to the environment but also to the spirit and to God.

THE PERSONA

The way in which we adapt to society is dependent on one aspect of our personality, which Jung called the persona. In ancient times this was actually the name of the mask worn by actors. The persona is that aspect of our self that we want to present to the outside world. Social adaptation and success depend on the quality of the persona. If your persona adapts easily to new situations, while at the same time reflecting the valid and real ego qualities that it covers, then you should be able to adapt to the world around you and manage change. Problems arise when, for various reasons, we try to adopt a persona that does not fit. Initially the persona is said to develop out of the changes and expectations of others around us—parents, teachers, media, and the world. We all know that children quickly learn which behaviors are seen as desirable and which are not. The desirable traits therefore become part of the persona while behavior characteristics which are seen to be socially unacceptable tend to become repressed and deeply hidden within the unconscious. Jung called these hidden parts the shadow.

Through our dreams we can start to tap into the unconscious parts of our psyche and learn to understand aspects of our persona and the hidden aspects of our shadow. Without the dream it would take longer and would be more difficult to identify the unique aspects of our persona and how we utilize them.

Maya was just fifteen years old when she hit crisis point and started to fear going to school and was spending more and more school days at home with her mom. Maya described herself as a "good girl, always doing the right thing, and trying to please everyone all the time." In her efforts to do this, it seemed that she forgot about herself all too often. She started to explore what this was about and came to a point where she realized that she felt worthless and had a very negative view of herself and her abilities and feared rejection by those who were closest to her. She thought that this feeling might be linked to her relationship with her mother and father. Through a series of significant dreams, she worked out that the "good girl" persona was quite a false one. Her dreams at this time centered on the circus, with vivid images of clowns, dazzling magicians, and people dressed up in mysterious costumes. These dreams seemed to tell Maya of false fronts, dressing up in order to be something you are not, and deception. Maya felt a sense of imbalance and seemed unable to keep the mask on any longer. Underneath her mask—in her shadow—Maya felt intense feelings of anger and rage against her parents and others around her. Through her dream and other work she managed to explore these thoughts and feelings to some extent to unveil a little more of the self and to create greater harmony in her inner and outer worlds.

THE SHADOW

In Jung's view the two aspects of the personality, shadow and persona, balance each other. When this balance is tipped to one side, it can end up in an intense personality that is all shadow with no concerns for the outside world and what others think. On the other hand, all persona can result in a shallowness and overconcern with how others perceive us. The shadow can be compared to the Freudian notion of the unconscious: it may not always be conscious but it is always active. When aspects of the shadow touch our awareness they can bring feelings of guilt, shame, and fear of rejection. We can use defense mechanisms to avoid the painful feelings of the shadow and project them onto another person. At times of change we may be especially prone to this.

LEFT: *A reference to the shadow is found in the New Testament's story of Noah, depicted here in an illustration from the Nuremburg Bible. Water is often seen as a symbol of the unconscious, and the floods in this image represent the washing away of the persona.*

THE SHADOW AS MANIFESTATION OF CHANGE

Through shadow projection we are able to turn reasonable people into wicked people. At best this can lead to scapegoating. At worst this can lead to bigotry and prejudice against those who are different to us. Some Jungian theorists suggest that shadow projection lies at the root of all pogroms, massacres, and wars. Through such projection we can turn the other side into monsters rather than human beings. Adolf Hitler persistently referred to the term *untermenschen* (subhumans) to describe the Jewish people. Through the Nazi propaganda machine, it could be argued that he persuaded much of the German population to collectively project its shadow onto the Jews, homosexuals, and Slavs.

THE ANIMA AND ANIMUS

As previously discussed, through his study of dreams Jung suggested that everyone has some characteristics of the opposite sex, whether in physical or psychological form. Jung believed that the animus and anima developed through the process of human evolution. He argued that when these aspects of the psyche become involved with the shadow it can lead to contamination. When this happens feminine aspects of the psyche are experienced as bad and are repressed in the male, and vice versa. Jung also believed that the anima and animus can provide us with a way for working with inner and outer adaptation or change.

Change and growth

Jung's theories are founded on principles of growth, development, individuation, and self-realization. He saw the whole life cycle as a continual process of change and growth regulated by the self. Jung described the psyche as a highly efficient organ of adaptation. He attributed this to the fact that the evolution of the psyche occurs within the context of the evolution of the world. The psyche is pure nature. In Jung's thinking, principles of adaptation, homeostasis, and growth apply to the psyche just as they do to any other biological phenomenon.

Freud, rather like Jung, also developed early theories in the context of a biological approach. Over time, however, this tended to become more sociologically oriented. Originally Freud conceived of psychic energy as resembling a current, which when blocked overflowed into other organs. Freud believed we are all born with strong but unconscious instinctive drives that provide us with a fundamental motivation in life. He suggested that the key drives for personal survival are the sex drive and the self-preservation drive. As adults we are largely unaware of these drives—they remain within our unconscious worlds but can spur us into enacting certain behaviors. Tapping into our dream worlds can help us to raise our awareness about the nature of these drives. Once they are made conscious, we are better able to understand them and manage them.

Freud suggested that problems arise in the human psyche and functioning when the emotional energy associated with these drives becomes frustrated or punished. When we consider the need for change and adaptation from day one of our birth to the day of our death it not surprising that psychic problems are plentiful.

In the very beginning of life when children are taught to conform to the rules of the adult world their basic instincts inevitably become controlled and suppressed. For example, self-assertion is not usually encouraged in a child, as this generally does not accord with the powerful parents' needs and wishes. Any form of sexual expression is also discouraged in most cultures. The consequence of this repression is that the emotional energy that lies behind these drives becomes repressed and disowned rather than being channeled into socially acceptable forms.

However, as with Jung, Freud believed that repressed energy did not merely vanish. He believed that it remains at an unconscious level and usually seeks another outlet when the conscious part of the mind is not available to keep it down—when you are asleep, for example. This energy is then manifested in our dreams.

Throughout the life cycle humankind is adapting to its environment and dealing with changing demands, changing relationships, situations, and emotions. These changes can lead to internal psychic conflict and anxiety as we have to try to manage each new situation. Freud claimed that the ego tries to defend itself from the anxiety arising out of the conflicts created by desires which society may deem unacceptable. He put great store in the concept of repression as the key means for defense of the ego.

At each developmental stage of life the infant or young child is confronted with events and situations that challenge, or in some cases threaten, their ways of doing things or their instinctual drives. According to Freud such adaptation to change requires adjustments to take place in the id, ego, and superego. It is thought that if successful adjustments are made, then this can lead to personal growth. If the adjustments are unsuccessful, there can be some degree of stuckness.

New environmental demands are always going to be stressful for infants and young children. Even a seemingly small action such as putting a newborn infant to sleep in its own cot can be highly upsetting for them, as this means they have to learn to separate from their mother or the caregiver whom they depend on and know. Later in life toddlers have to adapt to separations, including being at nursery school and other social situations. As well as this there are all the unexpected changes that life may bring, such as death of someone close or a divorce. Some of theses changes can stifle a child's growth rather than enhance it. In some cases the child can become trapped at a certain stage of development, and then much of the later development is disrupted as a consequence.

Freud's daughter

Anna Freud (1895–1982), the youngest of Freud's six children, was also a prominent thinker in the world of psychoanalysis. She studied psychoanalysis with her father and then opened a practice next to his. They even shared the same waiting room. She developed and extended the concept of ego defense mechanisms and suggested that there was more to ego defense than repression. Her work on these defense mechanisms and other activities of the ego, particularly in the field of child development, gained her a distinct and separate reputation in the field of psychoanalysis.

Repression

Dreams provide an outlet for repressed material. If we are able to listen to our dreams and try to make some sense of them, we can gain valuable insights into our unfulfilled wishes and repressed emotions. According to Freud all ego development, self-growth, and adaptation to the environment are dependent on primary repression. Freud and his followers believed that in primary repression the initial emergence of an instinctual impulse is prevented. Secondary repression is said to involve the disguising of the manifestations of repression, so that these are kept unconscious. The return of the repressed consists of the involuntary appearance of the repressed unconscious into the conscious primary impulse.

Many people get confused between the concepts of repression and basic inhibition. Repression is thought to differ from inhibition in that it involves two elements of energy. First there is the energy that is put into the actual impulse that is struggling to be released and acted on. Secondly, there is the energy that is invested into holding back the impulse and maintaining that level of repression. Some theorists compare repression to a dam. This type of imagery can be very apparent in one's dreams. Images of bursting dams can tell the dreamer of the struggle of repression. In the bursting dam scenario the dreamer can experience two forces—the force of water pushing against the dam and the force of the dam holding back the water. The repressed material and the energy that is used to keep the material back are both illustrated within the imagery. Inhibition is often compared to switching off a light. Thus with a simple flick of a switch you can remove that which you didn't want to see. Dreams that involve items that disappear for no obvious reason may tell of the dreamer's inhibitions.

Although the word denial has come into every day usage, the Freudian concept of denial describes an extreme sort of self-protection that particularly occurs at times of sudden change. A person who denies a situation simply refuses to acknowledge its existence, and they actually have no idea that they are doing this.

Charles Rycroft in the *Critical Dictionary of Psychoanalysis* notes that a denial defense mechanism is that "by which either a) some painful experience is denied or b) some impulse or aspect of the self is denied." These two things are not the same. According to Freud, when painful events are denied this is connected to the pleasure principle and the denial becomes part of the process of wish fulfilment—like denying someone's death because you wish it had never happened. Dreams of a deceased loved one are common soon after their death or at times of anniversaries. Their presence in the dream can be quite vivid and real. Analysts often attribute this kind of dream imagery to the psychological process of denial, where the dreamer has not yet accepted the reality of the situation.

Projection is another psychoanalytic concept that can be useful for us when dealing with anxiety, or conflict. Projection can be thought of as attributing your own unacceptable beliefs and motives to someone else. For example, rather than admitting that you might hold an anxiety-provoking emotion like fear of change yourself, you can sometimes project this thought onto someone else. Then you may see the other as the angry or competitive one and this frees you to be good and protect yourself. Actually these feelings may be related more to yourself than to the other person.

RIGHT: *The story of Jekyll and Hyde is a perfect illustration of Jung's shadow theory—the hidden aspects of our psyche that conflict with our dominate persona. Robert Louis Stevenson's story is about Dr Jekyll, an intellectual bachelor obsessed with his shadow, who is eventually transformed into the monstrous Mr Hyde.*

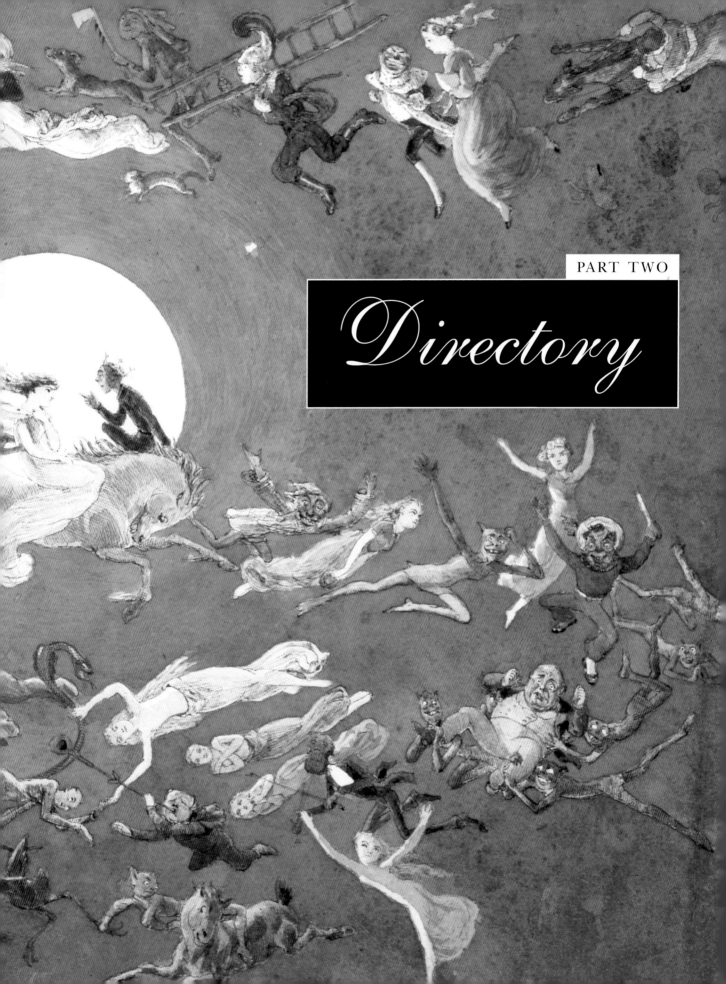

Directory

Common Items

PEOPLE OFTEN DREAM ABOUT COMMON ITEMS BECAUSE THESE OBJECTS ARE ENCOUNTERED DURING

THEIR WAKING DAY. THEY MAY COME INTO CONTACT WITH ONE ITEM OR PIECE OF EQUIPMENT MORE

THAN ANY OTHER AND THIS CAN EXPLAIN ITS APPEARANCE IN A DREAM. HOWEVER, MANY COMMON

ITEMS DO CONTAIN SYMBOLIC VALUES AND MAY REPRESENT FAR MORE THAN THEIR EVERYDAY FUNC-

TION. THE WAYS IN WHICH THESE ITEMS ARE USED IN DREAMS CAN BE OF GREAT SIGNIFICANCE, AS

COULD THE CONTEXT OR SCENARIO IN WHICH THEY APPEAR.

Campbell's

CONDENSED

Important! Add whole milk

NEW ENGLAND CLAM CHOWDER

NET WT.
10½ OZ. SOUP

MONEY

Money when it appears in dreams is often thought to be a signifier of emotional transactions. Giving money away may represent a generosity of spirit or kindness on behalf of the dreamer, or it might reflect the emotional ties that are incumbent upon them at present. Receiving money can signify the acceptance of emotional support, or the emotional needs of the dreamer, which may or may not be fulfiled at present. Borrowing money within a dream can be a warning for the dreamer to hold back if a major financial situation is on the cards. It is well worth exploring all aspects of any personal or business deal before going ahead. Signing a check or making a payment is generally regarded as a positive sign, indicating that certain plans are going to schedule. The notions of saving and investing may have practical or emotional implications. If they appear in a dream they may simply relate to the need to save for the future, or they may bear some reference to the need to prepare oneself emotionally for situations or relationships which need attention.

FOOD AND DRINK

Dreams about food and drink are often cited as positive messages, particularly if the dreamer felt replete at the end of a meal. A sense of satisfaction after eating and drinking can indicate an emotional stability. However, gluttonous eating may reflect the dreamer's need to receive more emotional attention, since however much they eat, they can't seem to get quite enough. Likewise, in dreams where there is not enough food to eat, or water to drink, the dreamer may be feeling that there is an emotional shortfall in their life. For Freud, dreams which featured fruit related to a woman's breasts or buttocks. In dreams where rich foods like chocolate or cream appear, the dreamer may be connecting with their more extravagant side. These dreams can have positive or negative connotations,

depending on how the dreamer reacted to eating these rich items. Likewise, where food or drink is being consumed at a great feast or banquet, it is worth trying to remember one's feelings during this scene. Was the opulence and luxury an enjoyable experience, or did you feel guilty that while you were living the high-life others were going without? If the foods in a dream are breakfast foods, such as cereals or toast, these may underpin the dreamer's attitude toward a new project or situation. It is worth recalling how these breakfast foods were eaten. Was there an atmosphere of calm and enjoyment, or was the meal rushed and hasty? This can have implications with regard to the way the dreamer is feeling about the new scenario in their life. When wine appears in dreams it is often associated with rituals such as births and marriages. Wine in dreams can point toward future announcements such as engagements before the word is out to people in general. Eggs in dreams can signify the life process or fertility. If an eggshell is broken, the dreamer may need to do some work in their waking life on breaking out of an emotional problem. Dairy products are often cited as yearnings or reflections on youth. Milk, with its connotation of breast-feeding, is often viewed as a symbol of the link between mother and child. Dreams of apples are often tied to the illicit apple in the garden of Eden, and are thus taken as signs of a misdemeanor or feelings of guilt.

The bitter taste of a lemon is related to bitter personal experience. Is this bitterness a residue from a past occurrence or is it part of an ongoing problem? Dreams involving bread are usually linked to money and the ability to provide for oneself or one's family. Christianity associates receiving our "daily bread" with the need for ongoing spiritual nourishment. Ice-cream dreams are sometimes taken as signs that the dreamer needs to be cool about a certain situation. Perhaps they have become over-excited about a project and need to take a step or two back in order to reevaluate it.

CUTLERY

Dreams of a shiny or glittering spoon are seen as messages that one's home life is running smoothly or according to plan. If the spoon is dirty, and you can't see your reflection in its surface, then aspects of your home life may need attention. Forks, especially when they are used for mixing or beating ingredients together, are often viewed as portents of social interaction. They may tell of occasions or events in the future, which the dreamer is anticipating with excitement. A rusty or twisted knife in a dream can relate to the dreamer's concerns regarding family problems or issues about their relationships with close friends. It is worth noting whether or not the knife was left in its broken state or if it was repaired.

GARBAGE

It is often said that dreams in which garbage appears are connected to our desire to rid ourselves of the negative or wasteful elements in our lives. However, if in the dream your garbage was being disposed of by friends or family members, then perhaps you are worried that your emotional burdens are resting too heavily on those who are closest to you. If you discover a valuable or precious item in a dream, then you may have just received or are about to receive some unexpected good news. If, on the other hand, you mistakenly throw out something valuable or precious, then possibly you are not appreciating someone close to you, or are simply taking them for granted. If you are covered in garbage, possibly you are afraid of some form of humiliation or you feel emotionally overburdened in your waking life.

JEWELRY

Jewelry dreams are seen by many to be symbols of wishes or wish fulfilment. Dream jewels often represent important events or ceremonies in the dreamer's life. At times, dream jewels are simply a representation of the dreamer's desire to accrue personal wealth, a better job or status of some sort. It is common to be driven beyond basic wishes by feelings of envy or greed. If jewelry is received in a dream, the dreamer may be experiencing a sense of recognition in their waking life, either for personal efforts or related to a work set-up. Viewing a rare jewel from a distance can be a sign that the dreamer has failed to understand an event or relationship in any meaningful way, and will need to put a lot of work in if they are to achieve a better understanding. Losing a jewel or having jewelry stolen may reflect the fears of the dreamer relating to financial or personal loss in their daily life. Diamonds appearing in dreams are usually associated with relationships. Their many faces imply that a relationship problem may have many

dimensions, and should be approached with extreme delicacy and sensitivity. Pearls are often taken to signify transactions of a financial nature, and may relate to a current business deal or aspect of one's personal financial affairs. Dream interpreters claim that rings are tied to aspects of the person's sexuality. They may reflect that the dreamer is currently unfulfilled sexually and is in search of more experience. More literally, rings can symbolize a desire to become more involved or committed to a present relationship, or the quest for some form of long-term partnership.

TOOLS

Dreams that feature tools are more often than not linked to masculinity and male sexuality. The phallic nature of many tools is often used as a justification for making this connection. However, in addition to this interpretation many claim that tools, with their capacity to dig and hide, are tied to elements that are hidden away in the memory of the dreamer. If tools in a dream are utilized for the purpose of levering items, the dreamer may be psyching themselves up for a period of personal growth or maturation. If the dream tool was a plow, the dreamer may be in need of turning over their emotional problems and searching for new angles to solve them. Corkscrews are taken to represent the uncorking of a new idea or plan. If the corkscrew was sluggish and unhelpful, then such a new embarkation may prove difficult or fruitless. If, however, the corkscrew worked with ease, then such a project may well be extremely successful. A dream spade may refer to something that is emotionally hidden. This may be an event or a memory tucked away in the dreamer's mind. The dream might either be imploring the dreamer to reopen this chapter in their life or could be telling them to leave whatever it is well buried. A spirit-level can be a sign that things are balancing

well in the dreamer's life, and little interference is needed in the present situation.

HOUSEHOLD ITEMS

Household items in dreams may simply show a dreamer's desire to own a particular piece of equipment, but their meanings can be a lot more significant. Dreams which feature brooms traditionally are seen as portents of good fortune. If the broom is damaged, the dreamer may be suffering from feelings of insecurity or low self-esteem. If the broom is one used specifically for outside jobs, it is worth looking at current plans and proposals. Are you taking too much notice of the outside world, instead of reflecting on what is really important to you? Dreams of scissors can be related to the cutting out of unwanted emotional aspects of the dreamer's life. If the scissors are unused in the dream, this may tell of a forthcoming emotional or romantic liaison. If the dreamer is already in a relationship, unused scissors can symbolize a desire for this relationship to grow stronger. Dream scissors can also be viewed as a sign that you are dividing your attention between too many projects or people. If you were using the scissors to cut, you may be in the process of making some very important decisions. Analyze if you achieved your cutting task successfully, or if the scissors were of no use to you. Dream envelopes often relate to the

conveying of messages, either from or to the dreamer. Open envelopes sometimes signify daily problems which can be tackled with no great effort. A sealed envelope can signify that a problem may be harder to solve than at first envisaged. If an envelope is bulging, the dreamer may be feeling that their waking life is overburdened either with worries about work or with the emotional expectations of those around them.

BOXES AND CONTAINERS

Dreams that involve boxes and containers are generally linked to the dreamer's psyche. These dreams may relate to feelings of safety, security, and containment. On the other hand, dream boxes and containers may signify that the dreamer is storing too much emotional baggage and needs to lighten their load. An empty box or container can be a sign that the dreamer is in need of emotional or practical fulfilment. If a dream box holds its contents with plenty of room to spare, the dreamer may be feeling comfortable in the way they are organizing their life and affairs, and are not feeling crowded in any way. If on the other hand, the box is overflowing with contents, this can symbolize a sense of being overburdened either with daily tasks or with emotions. It is worth remembering which dream items, if any, were offloaded in order to make the box easier to manage. A wallet or pocketbook con-taining personal effects may relate to the most private domain of the dreamer's world. Perhaps they are worried that someone has got too close to them or, on the contrary, they are seeking greater intimacy.

FURNITURE

Furniture in dreams can be related to the dreamer's state of financial or emotional security. Dreams of childhood furniture can be linked to feelings relating to our upbringing and to our parents, particularly if the furniture appears in the home within which we grew up. Freud believed that cupboards were representations of the female sexual organs and female sexuality. Moving furniture or attempting to squeeze it into a space which can't accommodate it, is usually taken as a sign of the manner in which one is trying to cope with emotional problems. If you manage to fit the furniture into the space, you may be feeling secure in your emotional life. If, however, the furniture does not fit, then you may be experiencing some form of emotional turmoil. Dreaming of a favorite sofa or armchair could be linked to the person who sits there most often, or who considers it their own place. Dreams that feature closed curtains can signify a sense that you can't face tackling a present issue in your waking life, and are trying to block it out. Such dreams can also be linked to your desire or need for secrecy relating to a particular issue. If the curtains are open in the dream, you may be feeling generous or ready to share some information with a special person or people. If the dream has a cushion in it, you may be wanting to protect yourself from someone or something. However, if the cushion formed part of a relaxation scene, then you may be feeling at peace with yourself or you may be particularly relaxed about a current situation or relationship.

Human Body

MANY DREAMS ABOUT THE HUMAN BODY ARE REFLECTIONS OF THE DREAMER'S FEELINGS ABOUT

THEIR OWN BODY. THESE DREAMS CAN BE SIGNIFICANT MARKERS OF THE DREAMER'S SELF-ESTEEM

REGARDING THEIR PHYSICAL APPEARANCE. IF IN THE DREAM THE BODY APPEARS TO BE ATTRACTIVE

AND HEALTHY, THEN THE DREAMER MAY BE FEELING CONTENT WITH THEIR OWN BODY. HOWEVER,

AN UNATTRACTIVE OR UNHEALTHY BODY COULD POINT TO SIGNS OF INSECURITY OR DOUBT THAT

THE DREAMER HAS REGARDING THEIR PHYSICAL APPEARANCE.

THE FACE

The face is usually the first part of a person's body noticed by the outside world, and as such the dream face may reveal the dreamer's feelings about the way in which they appear to others. A dream face may symbolize the way a person wants to be seen. On a more basic level, the appearance of a dream face may be a reflection of the dreamer's facial state on going to bed or waking up. If a beautiful dream face appears, this may be connected to feelings of honor or pride. The dreamer may be feeling self-satisfied about a particular issue at present, and believes their status is rising in social or work circles. If the dream face is completely unknown, this can signify changes in the dreamer's waking life. Note if there are any major changes in your life at present, and decide if you are handling them in the best possible way. If a dream face is being washed or cleansed, this can have links to emotions of guilt or sin. The act of cleaning may symbolize a desire for a fresh start, in order to move on from some act of wrongdoing. If a set of familiar or well-known faces are in a dream, then this can be a portent of future social events and possibly celebrations. It is worth trying to remember if the faces were just from your family group, or if they represent different spheres of your life. Lips in a dream are usually taken to represent the female genitalia, but are also connected to communication. They may act as a sign that you are not getting your message across and need to be more explicit in your communications. Dream mouths are loaded with sexual connotations, but are also linked to the idea of emotional nourishment. If the mouth was smiling, you may be feeling emotionally nourished, whereas a frown could indicate a need for greater support. An elderly face may simply be your projection of life in the future. However, aged faces also carry symbolic ties to the notions of wisdom and longevity. Dream beards are often associated with masculinity or, if the mouth is visible, with the female side of a man's nature.

EYES

Traditionally eyes have been considered as the link to the true soul of a person. They are said to be the windows through which one can spy a person's real psyche. In ancient times, philosophers claimed that eyes were the symbol of faith and belief. Therefore, in dreams, eyes are generally said to reveal the dreamer's attitude to and understanding of the world. Clear, strong eyes are said to reveal good insights and a clear perception of what is happening around us, whereas eyes with little or no vision are seen as symbols of an inability to make sense of the world. Furthermore, warm or smiling eyes are viewed as symbols of inner peace or contentment, while concerned or worried eyes reveal isolation or the need for greater communication. If the dream eyes are particularly focused, this can indicate a clarity of purpose on the part of the dreamer. They may be revealing the clear sight the dreamer has demonstrated when preparing a piece of work or a project. Eyes that are cloudy are often taken to represent fears concerning one's financial well-being and the possible need for advice in this area. If an eye is injured or diseased, this may have links to the notion of reputation. Consider your own reputation at present. Are you comfortable with the way people see you, or do you fear someone is plotting to undermine you or "talk you down"? Eyebrows are said to reflect dignity and

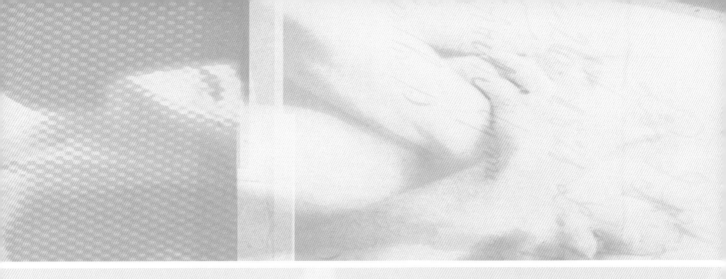

honor, and could indicate the fact that you are about to be recognized or appreciated by an unexpected source. If hair is being shed from the dream eyebrows, you may be worried about the way in which others view your status. Eyelashes are seen to represent secrets or secretive pursuits. Consider a secret you are holding at present. Do you need this to remain hidden from others, or is it time to share it with someone whom you trust? If a dream eye is wide and open like that of a young child, this can refer to innocence or the excitement caused by a new undertaking. Narrow eyes, on the other hand, may be a symbol of deceit or cheating. The tone of eyes can also be significant. Darker eyes are linked to emotional or romantic relationships, whereas pale eyes are seen as connectors to the more social side of one's world.

BREASTS

Dreams about breasts are often sexual dreams, but they may also be linked to feelings associated with motherhood or one's relationship with a mother or mother figure. Breasts may represent a time of personal growth or change in your life, or could refer to a period of enlightenment in some sphere. Breasts can also be seen in a negative light, as they may imply that you are too closely connected to your mother or mother figure, and that it may be time to strike out on your own and achieve a greater level of independence. Dream breasts can also refer to the idea of mother earth. In this case, consider how you are feeling about your own world at present, and assess if any changes are necessary. If you dream that you are resting your head on someone's breast, this can reveal that you are ready to form or consolidate a long-lasting relationship in either the social or romantic sphere. Voluptuous breasts can refer to the potential for good times ahead, whereas small or wrinkled breasts can foretell hard times.

BUTTOCKS

Buttocks are a very common dream symbol and have various interpretations. Such dreams may be sexual in nature and if they are, try to make an association with the person in the dream to discover if it was in any way significant to your own sexual desires. If clothes are shed from the buttocks in a dream, this may underline feelings of guilt, shame, or the risk of some form of humiliation. If you hit or kick someone else's buttocks in a dream, this can be a sign that you intend to rise up the career ladder or are seeking an imminent promotion. If, however, you try to kick someone's buttocks but miss, then you may be facing a range of difficult obstacles when launching a new project. Animal buttocks in dreams have traditionally been linked to notions of wealth and financial security. If more than one pair of buttocks appears in a dream, this may foretell of enjoyable social occasions or unexpected gatherings.

EARS

Ears in dreams are often a sign that the dreamer is either in need of better listening skills or in fact needs to be listened to. Such dreams may also be about the need for the dreamer to listen to their own true feelings and make a connection with their unconscious self. Dream ears can also reveal a concern on the part of the dreamer that someone close to them is not

being totally straightforward, and is holding back an important piece of information. If in a dream you possess more than two ears, you may well be feeling valued and respected by those around you, especially in a work situation. If you have the ears of an animal or a wild beast, you may be concerned that someone is lying to you or trying to act out some type of deceit. The size of ears in a dream can have important interpretive connotations. Tiny ears can reveal that someone has been lying to you, while very large ears can symbolize the help of a colleague or friend who to date has been of little or no assistance. Washing ears in a dream can be seen as a sign that good news is on the horizon. If someone else was washing your ears, then the good news may arrive from an unexpected quarter. Ears being pulled can represent an argument in the working part of your life. If there is an ongoing dispute, perhaps it is time to find a sensible and agreeable solution.

BLOOD

Blood in dreams is often seen as a representation of the life process itself. Blood is also linked to the ideas of rejuvenation and strength. The redness of blood bears historical connections to love, passion, and anger. Thus such dreams can be messages of strong personal feelings either of a very positive nature, or of an aggressive and antipathetic variety. A blood transfusion in a dream can symbolize that a current problem is on the verge of being sorted out. If blood is lost in a dream, the dreamer may be suffering either physically or morally. The circulation of blood in a dream may reveal that you feel a lack of personal strength, that life in general is flowing away. If the blood moved comfortably around a body, then your life may be running smoothly. However, if the path of blood is blocked, then life may not be going according to plan. If clothes in a dream are bloodstained, a person at work may be attempting to derail a project which is dear to you. If the blood is hemor-

rhaging, it's possible that the dreamer feels exhausted or drained in some way. If there is blood on your own hands in a dream, this may be an indicator of powerful feelings of guilt or shame about something you have done or are considering doing.

TEETH

Many people have dreams involving teeth, and many dream interpreters see teeth as symbols of the dreamer's self-respect. A very common dream involves witnessing one's own teeth falling out, which is generally cited as a symbol of the dreamer's fears of the ageing process or worries about the way others are perceiving the dreamer at present. If the dream teeth are completely rotten, then a current relationship may be on the verge of ending. Teeth which glisten or are especially clean, are linked to financial security or strong friendships. If a row of teeth are particularly straight or perfectly set, this may be connected to the strength of a family or friendship group. If the roots of the teeth are featured, you may be thinking about the stability of your waking relationships. If the roots are healthy, you are content about these, whereas twisted or unhealthy roots can signify concerns in this area of life. If you dream you are brushing your teeth, you may have recently given a sum of a money to a friend or to a family member. If a dream tooth is pulled out, this may be a warning not to act hastily in a

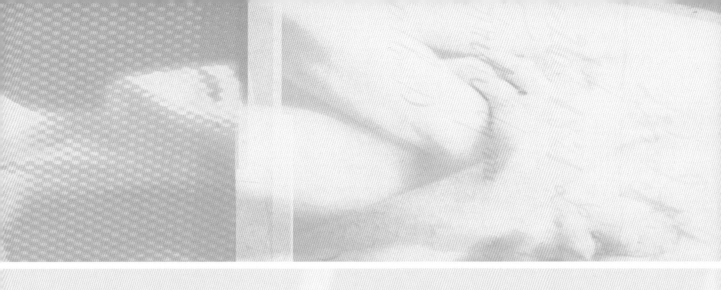

work-related matter. Before you act, it is worth considering the situation again in the light of any new information. If an object is lodged between two teeth, then a problem which seemed impossible to solve may soon be facing a realistic solution. Where one tooth is far larger than the rest of the teeth in a mouth, you may be worried that something in your personal or working life is going to turn out to be a great disappointment.

HAIR

Hair is historically associated with inner strength and the potential for personal growth. If the hair is in good condition, the dreamer may be feeling vital or strong, whereas hair in a bad condition can reveal feelings of low self-esteem or a lack of strength. If the hair is overly perfumed, this can be linked to the idea of the dreamer's vanity. If you applied the perfume yourself, then perhaps you are acting in an arrogant fashion about something in your life. If the hair is knotted or tangled, you may be experiencing a series of difficult problems or issues in your waking life which you need to smooth out. If the hair in the dream proves to be totally unmanageable, you should possibly reconsider the angle from which you are approaching a problem at present. Perhaps it is time to look at it afresh and see if there is another way to solve it.

If your hair is cut in a dream, this traditionally represents a symbol of success or an achievement in a new project. If you are cutting someone else's hair, this may be warn you to be on your guard in relation to anyone around you who acts negatively toward you.

HANDS

If in a dream hands are being stroked or comforted, this may relate to friendship or romance that you are involved in. If the hands are unclean, perhaps you are behaving in an inappropriate manner in some part of your life and you need to think about cleaning up your act. If the hands were flexible and useful, you may be experiencing some degree of success in your waking life, perhaps in your career sphere, whereas hands which are difficult to manipulate can underpin a frustration or a lack of direction.

FEET

Feet in a dream are usually taken as a sign of progress in the dreamer's waking life. If you or another person is bathing your feet, this could imply that you are keeping a safe distance from a current problem and will return to it when you are feeling better able to tackle it. You may be feeling dissatisfied or unhappy about that particular problem. If many feet are walking alongside each other, you may be concerned about money matters, and might need to double-check a situation before you part with any money. If the feet are marching forward powerfully, this can link to feelings of purpose and confidence underlying a current project. Slow-walking or lazy feet, on the other hand, can reveal ambivalence or uncertainty about where you are going. Therefore, the strength or the determination of your dream feet may indicate how you are approaching a certain task.

People & Characters

RELATIVES, FRIENDS, COLLEAGUES, NEIGHBORS OR SOCIETAL FIGURES FREQUENTLY VISIT OUR DREAM

WORLDS AND THEY ARE OFTEN CONCRETE REPRESENTATIONS OF DAILY LIFE. IN ANALYZING DREAM

MEANINGS, HOWEVER, IT IS WORTH CONSIDERING THE *SYMBOLIC* INTERPRETATIONS OF THESE FIGURES.

THEY CAN BE CONNECTED TO HIDDEN OR REPRESSED ASPECTS OF OUR PERSONALITIES. THEY CAN

RAISE ISSUES THAT WE WOULD RATHER FORGET. IF WE LISTEN TO OUR DREAM CHARACTERS, THEY

CAN HELP US DEAL WITH CONFUSION AND CONFLICT OR ACHIEVE BALANCE IN OUR WAKING WORLDS.

WHATEVER THE CASE, IN ORDER TO ACHIEVE A MEANINGFUL UNDERSTANDING OF DREAM CHARAC-

TERS, IT IS IMPORTANT FOR THE DREAMER TO CONSIDER THE ATMOSPHERE, THE ROLE THAT EACH

CHARACTER PLAYED, THE FEELINGS THAT WERE EXPERIENCED WITHIN THE DREAM, AND OUR WAKING

ASSOCIATIONS TO THESE PEOPLE.

MOTHER

Interpretations of mother-based dreams will largely depend on the dreamer's relationship with their mother. Is the relationship riddled with conflict and tension? Is the relationship envied by other family members or is it close and trouble-free? Some dream analysts suggest that dreams of your mother may be connected to the intuitive, creative, and instinctive aspects of your inner self. A dream about your mother may also be communicating unconscious thoughts and feelings that you have toward her. It can symbolize mixed feelings associated with separation and attachment. Psychological independence from one's mother is generally seen as a sign of maturity and growth. If there is a conflict with the dream mother, this may point toward the dreamer's need to resolve tensions between dependence and independence. Other interpretations of the dream mother center on feelings of loss and mourning for childhood and a longing for the safety of the primary relationship.

FATHER

Particularly for men, the appearance of a dream father can represent emotions that surround authority and power. Dreams of fathers can also be linked to feelings of growth and suggest the need for the dreamer to develop their independence and assert their own power in the world. If the father figure appears to be dead in the dream, this may indicate feelings of hostility toward the father and could be associated to unresolved anger toward him. In some instances, perhaps more for women than men, father dreams are connected to notions of protection and safety. Such dreams may also be a sign for the dreamer to make contact with the male side of their personality. If your father was absent from your childhood life, then a dream of him may be raising unanswered questions for you which you may want to explore.

Jung gives the example of a dream of a young man he worked with. In this dream the young man sees his father as a drunken driver who ends up smashing his car into a wall. This image was completely contradictory to the waking perception that the man had of his father, who was law abiding and highly respectable. Jung suggested that this son was overly in awe of his father. He proposed that the dream symbolized the unconscious "dethroning" of the father. By reducing the father's power and respectability in his dream, the son would be able to move toward achieving a whole sense of self as a person in his own right. He could then start to take on the emotional and practical responsibilities of adult life.

BROTHER/SISTER

Many, although not all, dreams about a brother or sister represent some symbolic aspect of the self. It is important to decide whether this is the case before making any interpretation. A brother or sister who appears in your dream may represent an aspect of your other self. This is what Jung called the "shadow." He argued that the other aspect of ourselves—the part that we do not present to the world—emerges in our dreams, often in the form of a brother or sister. By listening to our dreams we can work on this unconscious part of ourselves

and bring it into our conscious awareness to enrich our waking experiences. When a female dreams of a brother or a male dreams of a sister, Jung called this our "soul image." A female who dreams of her brother is raising the profile of the masculine side of her personality (her animus). When a male dreams of his sister Jung suggested that this represented his anima (female side). The image that represents the animus or anima may be the opposite type to what the dreamer appears to be in waking life. For example, if you see yourself as a gentle and soft woman, the animus may be an aggressive, hard-nosed character. In brother/ sister dreams this missing or repressed part of our personality is coming to the fore.

GRANDMOTHER/GRANDFATHER

These age-old archetypal figures can represent notions of wisdom, knowledge, power, and understanding. If a grandmother or grandfather appear in your dream you may want to listen to their points of view and take heed to their advice. Sometimes dreams of these characters may be overwhelming and you may feel subsumed and struggle to prevent them from engulfing you. Jung called these figures "mana personalities," meaning the divine or holiness. Jung argued that a man or woman who becomes possessed with the grandmother or grandfather figure may become convinced that they have superior insights or greater wisdom than the rest of the world. He suggested that rather than repress or project this aspect of the self, it is best to work on it and try to integrate it into your consciousness. Freud, however, suggested that the Great Mother figure is less an abstract archetype and more connected to the dreamer's own individual representation of his or her mother. The mother can symbolize femininity and love, power and mystery. She can foster growth but at the same time she has the potential to be overpowering and domineering and can be responsible for stunting the growth of the dreamer.

visualization exercise

Try to recall your first childhood memory of your mother. Can you see what she was doing? What was she wearing? How did she look? Did she have a particular smell? Can you remember how you felt toward her? How closely does this image fit with the notion of the Great Mother archetype?

CHILD/BABY

Pregnant women often dream of babies and usually there is no abstract symbolism involved in these cases. In other instances, however, dreams of babies and birth often reflect notions of creativity and also point to new beginnings—this may be in work, home life, a new relationship or big journey. In this sense baby dreams are often quite optimistic. In other cases, dreams of babies and young children are often said to represent the childhood part of ourselves, especially the vulnerability of the dreamer and their unconscious desire to be looked after and nurtured. The connection with our infant selves can reawaken us and reduce some of the pain and difficulty of adult life.

Sarah's dream

Sarah worked in a small nursery with babies and young children. She recently had a spate of dreams about being pregnant and having a baby. In her most recent dream she actually kidnapped one of the babies with whom she works. This last dream was particularly worrying for Sarah and when she described it to her boss, Sarah was told not to tell anyone about it. When Sarah started to analyze this dream she talked about a forthcoming trip she was planning. Sarah had just recovered from a difficult relationship with an ex-boyfriend and had recently decided to take a year out and travel the world. She was both excited and apprehensive about this new phase of her life. In discussion, Sarah realized that this spate of baby dreams not only related to her everyday life of work but also connected to new beginnings. Sarah linked the kidnapping dream to her feelings of loss around her personal and professional life. The dream served as a reminder for her not to throw out the baby with the bathwater and to hold on to the good parts of the old world as she embarked on the new.

KING/QUEEN

Dreams of kings and queens often represent authority figures or people of power who inhabit the world of the dreamer. Such dreams may refer to parents, teachers, bosses or certain domineering friends. The dreamer needs to observe how they felt within the dream scenario. Did the dream induce feelings of passivity? Did you feel like a "subject" or were you represented as the powerful king or queen? Some analysts suggest that the appearance of a queen is connected to notions of intuition and to aspects of creativity and the anima. If a king and queen appear together in a dream, it may suggest aspects of harmony and balance within the conscious and unconscious aspects of the dreamer's world.

PRINCE/PRINCESS

Dreams of a prince or princess may represent a responsibility that you may be trying to consciously ignore. Other dream analysts suggest the appearance of a prince in one's dream is connected to the idea of wish-fulfilment. Perhaps you are hoping to achieve some new ambition. If you are unconventional or anarchic in your waking life, a dream prince or princess—establishment figures—may be sending you a message to be more conventional.

BRIDE/GROOM

Dreams of brides and grooms are often said to represent notions of unity and harmony within the world of the dreamer. In some instances, however, such dreams can symbolize the dreamer's feelings of envy in relation to the harmonious couple. In other instances the dream bride or groom may tell of wishful thinking on the part of the dreamer. It is worth noting the mood and role of the bride and groom within the dream scenario to achieve the most accurate interpretation. It may not necessarily be one of joy. The role of the feminine or masculine sides of the dreamer's conscious and unconscious world may be worth examining in relation to wedding dreams. For example, the dreamer may need to be more assertive in dealing with friends or they may need to pay more attention to their nurturing, feminine side right now.

PRIEST/RELIGIOUS LEADER

Dreams of spiritual or religious leaders are often associated with concepts of inner wisdom, and direction. If you dream of religious figures it may mean that you are in touch with the moral side of your psyche—you may be struggling with an ethical dilemma and searching for right and wrong. If there is a choice to face, a priest dream may be guiding you to listen to your inner voice. In other instances dreams of religious leaders may connect to feelings of oppression, and guilt. The interpretation of a religious dream will be connected to the dreamer's experiences, thoughts, and feelings surrounding religious leaders. Are they positive, negative, or unresolved?

TEACHER, JUDGE, POLICE

Authority dream figures often appear to guide us or sometimes to impose themselves on us. Often they will be some kind of reflection of our parents. How these characters are manifested can give us clues to address responsibilities that we might prefer to sweep under the carpet. The appearance of a teacher may be guiding you toward some aspect of learning—either in relation to your personal development or further study. Judges and policemen usually allude to aspects of the establishment. If in waking life you see yourself as one who flouts authority, then you may need to moderate this.

HERO

The hero we dream of may not be a concrete representation of that person but rather may embody all that we admire about humankind. For some the hero may represent an inner self that we aspire to be. In fairy tale mythology the hero usually has to overcome great struggles to reach his final destination on a long journey. The end of his quest usually results in him saving another person who is less fortunate and courageous than himself. This may be something that you are striving for yourself or you may be feeling the need to protect others who are close to you. The modern-day hero may be represented by a politician, a scientist, an athlete or even a pop star. If a hero appears in your dream, notice who they were and how they looked. Most importantly try to make connections between your associations with that person in your conscious life to give yourself clues to what you may be striving for and why.

THE SHADOW

Dark and sinister figures can often frequent our dreams. They may appear as an actual shadow or they be more subtle evil dream characters. Jung referred to the shadow as the dark side of ourselves that we would like to keep hidden—"the thing a person has no wish to be." The shadow can be thought of as an instinctive primitive side of our personality that we might try to repress. It can take the form of an advisor who guides us on the journey of life. It can appear as a dangerous character such as a murderer or an assailant. If a sinister figure appears in your dream, try not to shy away from it. Notice how these characters controlled the dream. Observe if any aspect of you may be contained within the shadowy figure and, if so, address some of the negative emotions that are being raised for you. Did the dream describe your private but perhaps shocking urges?

Places

DREAMS OF DIFFERENT PLACES CAN OFTEN TELL OF THE INNERMOST FEELINGS, HOPES, AND FEARS

OF THE DREAMER. WHERE DREAM PLACES ARE FAMILIAR, SUCH AS A CHILDHOOD HOME OR A HOLIDAY

DESTINATION, THE MESSAGES MAY BE ONE OF LONGING FOR THE PAST OR ACKNOWLEDGING YOUR

INNER CHILD. BUILDINGS MAY REPRESENT THE BODY OR PERSONALITY OF THE DREAMER OR

SOMEONE CLOSE. IN ANY DREAM OF PLACE OR SITUATION IT IS IMPORTANT TO NOTICE YOUR WAKING

ASSOCIATIONS WITH THAT DREAM. IT WILL BE DIFFERENT FOR EACH PERSON AND YOUR

CONSCIOUS CONNECTIONS TO THE DREAM IMAGE MAY GREATLY INFLUENCE THE WAY YOU

UNDERSTAND THE DREAM.

BUILDINGS

Dreams of buildings often tell us of feelings we hold about ourselves or a loved one. In other instances they can represent ideas about a higher intellect or understanding. If we are exploring parts of a building in the dream, this may be a metaphor for our need to explore different aspects of our own potential, whether that is in relationships, work or our own self-development. If the dream building is familiar in some way but we discover unknown rooms, then it is likely that this dream is telling you of untapped inner potential that needs to be harnessed.

HOUSE

A dream of your house may simply be a representation of yourself. It may represent your self-image or how you hope to present yourself to the outside world. Notice how your dream house looked. Was it ostentatious and highly decorated? Was it simple and cosy? If the house was falling apart, it may be a sign for you to do some repairs in your waking world. Perhaps you need to look after yourself a little. To go upstairs in the dream house may mean that you are rising to greater intellect, actually going up to the head. To go down into the basement of the house could represent hidden aspects of the unconscious that may be repressed. If the house if full of clutter or people, it may be a sign for you that life is too busy and overcrowded right now and you may need to cut back. However, if the dream house is empty and bare, you may need to redress the balance and fill up your empty world in some way. Where doors or windows appear in the dream building, they may represent openings of some kind. This could be an opening within the body or an opening for escape. You may need to escape from the window or door to find a better place for yourself. Stairways are often thought to have a sexual basis, although there could be a more general interpretation of ascending

stairs as being connected to ideas of progress and ambition. Walls in houses support the whole building, so if they were crumbling or in need of repair, it may be useful to examine the fabric of your own life. A chimney in a building may be a phallic symbol, whereas an entrance may be a female sexual reference. Kitchens are usually centers of activity and are the heart of a home. There is usually a great deal of emotional and physical energy to be found in the kitchen. If this room appears in your dream, it is worth noting what your position was within the kitchen. Was it too hot for you on an emotional or physical level and, if so, were you able to get out? Bedrooms are usually places of comfort and intimacy. If you dream of a bedroom in the house this might perhaps be an expression of your feelings of security and comfort about your world. Alternatively, you may be able to identify some element of longing in the bedroom scene. In this case, perhaps you are hoping for a more stimulating sexual relationship.

PALACES AND CASTLES

If the building in your dream was a palace, notice its level of decoration and grandeur. Perhaps this dream is a statement about the way you wish to live or how you hope to project your image to the outside world. Were there lots of servants in the palace or were you alone? How did you feel in there? You may have felt completely out of place or

you may have realized that you really do belong there. A dream of a castle may have similar connotations. It is important to notice whether your castle was a safe place. Perhaps it was surrounded by a moat or it may have been under attack. You may need to retreat from some kind of personal threat or attack on your world. If so, try to address this issue in waking life as best as you can and listen to your dream message.

GARDENS

Some analysts suggest that a dream garden is in fact a symbol of your true self. If the garden is overgrown and disordered, it may be a symbol of the chaos of your psyche or your world right now. However, if the garden is thriving and has an abundance of lush vegetation and healthy flowers, then it could be that you are thriving on all levels. If a pond or fountain is in your dream garden, it may symbolize a source of new life or creativity. You may be working on a new project or developing new aspects of your personality. Notice whether there is grass in your garden. If so, did it need to be cut back or was it neatly trimmed? Some dream analysts say that grass is connected with your free time in waking life, as cutting the grass is something that we may do on a leisurely sunny afternoon. If you were collecting grass to make hay, the dream may be telling you to make the most of current opportunities before it is too late.

PARTIES AND CLUBS

The biggest insight into the meaning of these dreams will be how you felt at the party or club. Parties and clubs are places where we would like to feel a sense of security. We are probably with like-minded people, friends, and family. However, sometimes we may feel isolated at a party—we may feel stuck for words or different and unable to socialize. Notice how you felt at your dream party. Were you the life and soul who held it all together? Were you hosting the party? Or did you feel excluded? Answers to these questions may show how you are feeling in your relationships with those around you. You might be looking for greater support from those you love or you might be trying to create your own individuality and stand out from the crowd.

CINEMA

If a cinema appears in your dreams, you may looking for a bit of escapism. You may yearn for a life overseas or for some action-packed adventure. If you see a film in your dream, then it will probably have been carefully selected by your unconscious rather than being a random choice. If the dream film was full of adventure and excitement, your dream may be telling you that you need to spice up your life in some way. Similarly if it showed a romantic encounter, perhaps you should try to address this aspect of your waking life.

WORKPLACE

Dreams of being in your workplace may be connected to feelings that we have about stability. A workplace can be associated with an atmosphere of high productivity. On the other hand, a place of work can mean feelings of boredom, and lack of self-fulfilment. Notice how the workplace in your dream felt to you. If your workplace was busy and overcrowded, it may suggest that you feel overwhelmed by too many demands.

A closed office door can tell of something missing. Dreams of office tension can indicate a fear that trouble may be ahead. Some analysts say that dreams of working hard in your workplace signal positive change in your love life.

Maggie's dream

I dreamt that I was sitting typing at my desk as always. It was a grey and rainy day outside. People were coming and going, when all of a sudden my computer just stopped working. But it didn't just crash like it would normally—it slowly transformed itself. The keyboard became like the black and white keys of a piano and the screen became sheet music. Then as I was typing the most beautiful orchestral music came out of some speakers. It was like I was playing for the whole orchestra even though I can't play an instrument. Just as I was coming to the end of the first movement some of the guys came out of their rooms to find out what was going on and they saw me at the keyboard. I finished my piece and came to a dramatic ending and got up to bow. Instead of clapping as I had anticipated, they just all turned around mumbling to themselves and went back to their offices.

What do you think Maggie's dream is telling her? Perhaps she feels unappreciated in her current job, illustrated by the lack of applause. She may be harboring a desire to explore her creative side.

THEATER OR CONCERT HALL

The theater is often said to be an examination of real life. A theater dream may give the dreamer some insight into their unconscious projections about their waking life, especially within a social context. Dreams of performing are usually connected with ideas about our own self-image and our desire to project that image. On stage we may be performing as we do in our social lives. We may be looking for praise and applause.

Such dreams may tell of a desire to be loved and admired by those around you. The dream audience usually represents those who surround us—like friends and family. If you dream of a theatrical audition, it may be an expression of worry about being tested in some part of your life. This may be in an actual test or job interview, or it may refer to something less obvious such as being tested in a new relationship. If you or other dream characters are wearing stage make-up, then you may be concerned about being deceived in some aspect of your waking life.

COURTROOM

Assuming that the dreamer has not actually committed a crime, a courtroom scene may have several interpretations. If you were on trial, the dream may be expressing your own inner feelings of guilt about some wrongdoing you may have committed. If you were the judge in the scene, perhaps you crave some kind of authority. Dream judges may also tell of decisions that need to be made by yourself or by someone around you. Courtrooms are generally connected to notions of establishment and authority, so it is useful to consider how you reacted to the courtroom scene. This may help to give you some indication about your inner feelings toward authority. Did you feel rebellious and naughty? Or did you rather feel triumphant and proud to be part of the powerful establishment?

PRISON

It is important to consider who was in prison in the dream. If it was someone else, this may not necessarily refer to that person. Rather it may be some aspect of yourself and your psyche that you have repressed and kept locked away. Sometimes this may be connected with an episode that occurred in childhood, but which needs to be released and given some conscious attention in waking life. If you were in the dream prison, it is likely that you feel trapped in some aspect of your life. Dreams of prisons may also relate to our own need to inflict punishment on ourselves. Sometimes we may inflict punishment for crimes not yet committed or actions that we may have carried out without thinking. Such a dream symbol may often be out of proportion to the deed.

interpretation tips

What was the prison cell like? Were there bars on the windows and locks on the doors? Who was guarding? Were there other inmates and, if so, do you know why they were there? Did you feel threatened or quite safe in prison? Did you escape or were you there forever? What were your feelings before, during, and after your prison stay? Was there light at the end of the tunnel? Did you think that you deserved to be there? Did you give support to others around you or were you supported by others?

SCHOOL

If you appeared in school in the dream, the interpretation of its meaning will largely depend on your attitude to school in real life. Many people hated their schooldays and if this is the case, a dream about school may be connected with the inner pain you suffered during that time. In many ways the shadow of those times may still be hanging over you and the appearance of school in your dream may provide you with a chance to process and work through feelings of anguish and distress that you have kept under wraps. Some dream interpreters suggest that dreams of schools or other academic institutions such as universities and colleges tell of your need to develop new intellectual territories for yourself. Perhaps you need to study a new subject or take up a new hobby. A dream of a particular teacher may be connected to your intense feelings about that person—either positive or negative. A dream teacher may also symbolize a particular authority figure who appears in your waking life now, perhaps a manager or an older relative. A dream in which you see yourself playing with children at school can have a dual meaning. It could mean that you are enjoying playing with life right now, or it could be telling you to stop taking life so seriously and take some time to relax and find your playful side. You should be able to recognize which interpretation best suits you right now.

AIRPORT

Airports as a place for departure to far-away places may symbolize your desire to travel or escape some aspect of your life. Perhaps it is time for you to leave a job or relationship and find new destinations. In an airport dream the foreign destinations could also represent aspects of your unconscious that need to be explored in some way. Perhaps the dream is signaling that the time is right for you to do this in order to further develop aspects of your psyche and work out your true identity.

Journeys

MAKING A JOURNEY WITHIN A DREAM CAN BE A DIRECT REPRESENTATION OF A REAL JOURNEY THAT

HAS EITHER BEEN TAKEN OR IS ABOUT TO BE EMBARKED UPON. HOWEVER, IN MANY CASES THE

DREAM JOURNEY IS A SYMBOL OF THE DREAMER'S TRAVELS THROUGH THEIR OWN WORLD. JOURNEYS

WITH THEIR PROMISE OF DISTANT LOCATIONS ARE ALSO OFTEN CONNECTED WITH IDEAS OF

ESCAPISM OR SEARCHING FOR NEW CHALLENGES AND ADVENTURES IN THE DREAMER'S LIFE. JOURNEY

DREAMS CAN ACT AS A MESSAGE TO THE DREAMER, SUGGESTING THAT IT'S TIME TO TAKE NOTE OF

NEW POSSIBILITIES AND REACH OUT FOR NEW CHALLENGES.

CARS

Cars make frequent appearances in people's dreams, and with their capacity to be steered or accelerated they often represent the dreamer's drive in life. If the dreamer was driving the car and the journey was going smoothly, this can indicate a sense of contentment and control over the way their life is moving. If however, the dreamer found it hard to control the car, then they could well be feeling a sense of frustration with their situation or an inability to steer their life on a preferred course. If a dream car crashes, this might reflect disputes in the workplace or signs of conflict between the dreamer and someone in authority. Recall who was at the scene of the crash and how they helped you. This might have implications for the way you resolve conflict in your waking life. It is also important to consider the destination to which you were driving. Did you ever get there, and if you did, how did you feel at the journey's end? Were you elated at finally making it, or were you let down by the anticlimax of the final destination? Men's and women's dreams of cars are said to reflect different aspects of their psyche. For men, the dream car is generally thought to be linked to their ambition, masculinity, and in particular to their sexuality. For women, cars in dreams are thought to reveal the more ambitious side of their natures, and possibly represent their desire to get on in life and perhaps even to propel themselves into the fast lane. If when driving a dream car, you are journeying along a long open highway, this may indicate feelings of liberation or suggest that you are looking forward to some form of freedom, such as leaving a job or retiring. If there is someone in the back seat of the car, insisting that you drive a certain way or in a certain direction, then consider the possibility of a person in your life who is trying to dictate too much to you, either in a work setting or in a domestic context.

BOATS

For many dream analysts, dream boats are imbued with positive messages, linked to the idea of finding good things over the horizon. Boats are also said to represent periods of change in a person's life, as they move from one set of scenery across the water to another. The conditions of travel are seen to be of significance. Calm and peaceful waters or seas can indicate a period of smooth change in the dreamer's life, whereas choppy or rough sailing conditions can mean that changes will be fraught with obstacles. The dream boat may also signify how you are feeling about the security of your social or family life. A safe vessel may show you are contained and happy in your personal life, whereas a damaged boat can mean you are concerned about certain relationships. If you are paddling on a small boat in a calm backwater, this could imply a sense of success with a particular project you are leading. If you are walking on the deck of a boat and admiring an ocean view, this can foretell of future times to be enjoyed. If a boat is drifting aimlessly on the water, the dreamer may feel disconnected from their world, and be drifting in life without clear direction. It may be a message for the dreamer to focus on what their real priorities are. If a dream boat capsizes, the dreamer may fear some imminent danger, and steps may need to be taken to avoid this danger.

BUS

As with other forms of transport, dream buses are often linked to the dreamer's direction in life. If the dreamer is the driver or a passenger this can also be tied to notions of control over one's own destiny. If you wait for a long period of time at a bus stop, this can reveal feelings of frustration, and a desire to move on with something at a quicker pace than you are achieving at present. A double-decker bus in a dream can symbolize the many levels of a problem, and the possible need for the dreamer to consider this problem from more than one angle. If you are driving a bus that contains friends or family members as passengers, you may be feeling a great sense of responsibility toward these people. If the bus ride was bumpy and unnerving, then you might be feeling a sense of unease about a project you are about to start.

TRAINS

Trains with their ability to enter tunnels are often connected to notions of sexual feelings, particularly if the passage is associated with feelings of elation or arousal. However, dream trains are also linked to notions of one's passage through life, and moving trains are often cited as a symbol of one's security about the way things are going at present in a personal or work setting. If the train is stuck on the platform at a station without any sign of moving, there may be a problem in one of your current plans that needs ironing out before any further progress can be made. If you are waiting for a train and the signs indicate that it's on time, this may signal a sense that things are running smoothly, but that you are reliant on others in addition to yourself for everything to go as smoothly as possible. If the train is forced to make an emergency stop, be wary that even though a project is moving along swiftly it may be derailed by a sudden interference or problem. If you are on a train which needs to stop at a railroad crossing, this might indicate the need for patience in one of your undertakings. If you bide your time with grace and goodwill, you may be even more successful than you had previously thought possible.

AIRPLANE

The flight path of a plane is usually associated with the dreamer's conscious or unconscious desire to fly away from a present situation. It can also represent the beginning of a new project, about which the dreamer is feeling particularly elated or excited. If you are the pilot of a plane and you appear to know what you are doing, this may well be tied to the idea of firmly taking control over a work project. You see yourself as the one to steer everyone else through this new beginning. If the dream plane is preparing to land or is actually on the runway, a current situation may be coming to a close. This can be a reflection of a social or romantic relationship, or could indicate that some business deal is nearly concluded. If the plane circles or hovers in the air, you may be experiencing a sense of aimlessness, perhaps wanting to land but unsure of what to do exactly to reach your stated goal. If you dream of a warplane, especially one that has bombs for releasing, you might be concerned about potential hurdles which you know are lying in your way. Reflect on where the warplane was and whether or not it released its bombs, and try to figure out solutions to the obstacles which lie in your path. If you are on a plane that is going out of control and are required to take over the control panels even though you have no flying experience, this can be a sign that others in a work or family setting are heavily reliant on you to lead them and alleviate their problems.

ROADS

Roads are usually linked by dream interpreters to life's journey. If the road is clear and straight, this can be seen as a sign of positivity and certainty on the part of the dreamer about their chosen life course. If, on the other hand, the road is long and winding, the dreamer may be feeling perplexed about their life course and worried about the complexity of their journey. If you are studying a complicated street map relating to a large town or city, you may be dealing with a set of complex issues in your waking life. A drive on a steep uphill road is seen as a reflection of struggle in your life. Perhaps at present, you are embarking on a strenuous section of your life's journey, and you are in need of that little bit of extra fuel or energy to get you to the top of the hill. If you are driving along a road, but are continually referring to a map, then you may be worried that you are being too reliant on the advice of others in your waking life. Maybe it is time to assert your own independence a little more. If you are confronted by multiple road signs all seemingly imparting different bits of information, then there may be a series of people trying to tell you differing messages, and you might need to follow your own instincts and be the one to make a choice. If a road is closed ahead and there is no way through, you might be feeling stuck in a relationship or work setting, and possibly need to talk directly to the person or the people involved about potential ways forward.

MISSED JOURNEYS

If you arrive late or miss a journey completely, this could simply be a reflection of your fears relating to timekeeping. However, such dreams are often symbolic of your worries about missing out in life, and of the need for vigilance and focus for you to stay on track. If you miss a journey because of your own disorganization, this may have implications for the manner in which you set about organizing your waking life. Perhaps it is time to take firmer control over your schedule and be more focused when setting down your plans. However, if you missed the journey because someone stopped you from getting there, this may reveal your worries about outside interference in your life, and the possibility that someone is in some way trying to impede your progress. If the missed journey is the result of a mishap or accident, this may reveal an inner desire to lay the blame for some wrongdoing or fault at someone else's door. If you experience anger or rage at missing the dream journey, you may be experiencing frustration or anger in your waking life. Possibly you have missed a job opportunity, or you have seen an idea of yours being successfully acted on by someone else. If you witness the means of transportation leaving and there is nothing you can do about it, this can imply you are concerned about not reaching your full potential in life.

LUGGAGE

Many dream analysts claim that luggage is a clear sign of the emotional baggage we transport around with ourselves. They also state that dream luggage can represent the deep issues that lie in the unconscious mind, which have yet to be opened and examined. If the bags are light, the dreamer may be carrying little emotional strain in their waking life. If, however, the bags are weighty and cumbersome, the dreamer may be feeling overloaded and burdened by emotional ties and problems in their real world. If you are carrying luggage in a dream, this may be a portent of a journey, real or emotional, that is about to take place. You may be planning a visit somewhere or be considering embarking on a new relationship. If you have lost your luggage, this can reveal a worry that you are not fully in control of a situation, and may need assistance in locating the missing pieces to solve a dilemma. Luggage can also be a symbol of matters in your life which you no longer require. Perhaps you need to move on from a certain friendship, or maybe it's time for you to start something that is completely fresh and challenging for you. If there is luggage for sale in a shop window, you may actually be associating yourself with the merchandise for sale. Perhaps it's time in a work context for you to be in the "shop-window" as you look for a new job and hope that an employer will spot your potential. If your dream luggage is securely locked and you are in possession of the key, this might be a sign that you are feeling particularly emotionally secure at present, and that your life is on an even keel. Dreams of losing a purse or wallet, with their very personal contents, can be indicators that the dreamer is concerned about shedding certain parts of their identity. It may also indicate that the dreamer has underlying fears that they need to reconnect with who they really are.

What dreaming does is give us the fluidity to enter into other worlds by destroying our sense of knowing this world... Dreaming is a journey of unthinkable dimensions, a journey that, after making us perceive everything we can humanly perceive, makes the assemblage point jump outside the human domain and perceive the inconceivable.

CARLOS CASTENADA

Communication

DREAMS ARE A UNIQUE FORM OF PERSONAL COMMUNICATION, AS THEY ARE A WAY FOR HUMAN

BEINGS TO COMMUNICATE WITH THEMSELVES. SOMETIMES THESE MESSAGES ARE OBSCURE AND

HIGHLY DIFFICULT TO INTERPRET. HOWEVER, IF THE DREAM ITSELF CONTAINS SOME OF THE SYM-

BOLS OF COMMUNICATION, ITS MEANING MAY BE EASIER TO DECODE. SOMETIMES THESE SYMBOLS

ARE ENTWINED WITH AN ARRAY OF OTHER DREAM SIGNS, BUT AT OTHER TIMES THEY STAND ON

THEIR OWN AS THE MAIN ITEM WITHIN THE DREAM SCENARIO.

LETTERS

Letters appear frequently in dreams, and on some occasions the entire contents of a letter can be read within the dream. Your anticipation of and attitude to the letter may be of significance. If you are excited about receiving the letter, then in your waking life you may be looking forward to hearing some positive news. If, on the other hand, you feel fearful about opening the envelope, then perhaps something in your waking life is bothering you, and you have not as yet had the courage to open it up and perhaps now is as good a time as any to confront the problem. If you are writing a letter within a dream, this may tell you of the need to communicate a piece of information to someone important to you. If you are writing a series of letters, then maybe there are several people who need to receive your communication. If someone is writing a letter to you, this can reveal your desire to be kept in the picture within a work situation. Did you get to see any of the text in this letter, and if so what bearing did it have on your everyday life? If the letter comes from a distant location, you may be considering travel or are thinking of someone who at present is in a different part of the globe. If the letter you see is written in indecipherable handwriting, it may be that someone is not clear enough in their communications with you, and you may need to ask them to be more explicit.

TELEPHONES

In dream interpretation, telephones are often cited as standard symbols for the "contacting" of the self. If you were speaking on the telephone, try to recall whom you were speaking to and what the conversation centered on. Perhaps you need to talk more fully with this person in your waking life. If you are scared of answering the telephone, it is possible that you are unwilling to listen to a piece of advice, or are not prepared to accept some criticism of yourself. If you repeatedly tried to dial a number but never succeeded in getting a connection, this may reveal an element of frustration within your life. Maybe a project is taking too long to get off the ground, or you are having trouble expressing your point of view. If a telephone rings continually in a dream but remains unanswered, there is a chance that you may be ignoring some problem or issue in your life by choosing to not hear it. If you reach a telephone box and there is no telephone within, then potentially you are missing a vital piece of information that would help when formulating a plan or proposal. If a larger than average telephone is featured by itself, this phone may represent yourself, and might be an indicator that you will soon be required to convey an important message. If you dream of a telephone answering machine, this may be tied to the notion of passing the buck or not accepting responsibility for some part of your waking life. Perhaps you are content to let others deal with a particular issue, when in reality it would be tackled in a much more successful way if you were the one who faced it.

E-MAIL/TEXT MESSAGES/FAX

These relatively modern methods of communication have been reported in many dreams, and are generally seen to represent the *faster* means of communication. If one of these appears in your dream, this may be a message concerning the need to attend to

some communication as soon as possible. Perhaps you have withheld some news from a family member, or a work issue which needs to be shared. Dreaming of these communication devices is often a positive sign, and represents your desire to move on speedily with a current project. However, it may also be a sign that you should be cautious when embarking on a new plan, and should not necessarily go with the initial premise. If you are too quick to jump at the first opportunity, you may not get to where you want to be. Dreams of telegrams are sometimes experienced by those who have a very positive or negative memory of receiving such a communication, particularly if it related to a significant life event, such as news of a birth, wedding or bereavement.

NOTICE/MESSAGE

Dreams featuring notices and messages are sometimes seen as wake-up calls to the dreamer, by stating that they aren't aware enough of the world around them. Perhaps the dreamer should be "taking note" of some element in their life. If the notice was pinned on a notice board, this may be relevant to your workplace, whereas if it appeared on a household item such as a refrigerator, then the message may be closer to home. If you are the one penning or sticking up the notice, this may either represent your need for greater emotional security, or show that you wish to communicate with

someone but have not yet found the right moment or method. If you are unable to decipher the notice even though others around you can read it, perhaps you are feeling left out of a particular social group or situation, or need to branch out into different social circles.

HANDSHAKE/GREETING

Handshakes are a common form of greeting in many parts of the world, and a dream handshake may be of significance to your waking world. If the handshake was strong and supportive, this might suggest that you are at present enjoying some element of balance in your life. If, on the other hand, the handshake was weak, then you may be feeling jaded about your situation or in need of an energy boost, either physical or spiritual, to improve the quality of your life. If someone offers their hand for a handshake but then withdraws it, maybe you are feeling distrustful of a particular person or feel that they may have done you some wrong. Try to remember who this person was, and analyze any possible significance to the reality of your waking world. Where the greeting was a hug, remember how you felt about this method of greeting. Was it a comfortable, warm experience, or did it feel uneasy and unnatural? In the former case, you may be in a situation where you feel appreciated and supported, whereas in the latter it may that you are feeling isolated or bereft of the necessary networks of support.

INTERVIEW

Interview dreams are extremely common, particularly among those who are waiting to discover if they have been granted an interview, or who are waiting for a real interview to take place. Such dreams may simply reveal your true fears and aspirations regarding the interview process or a particular interview situation. If you dream you are attending an interview, this may

mean that you are uncertain about the path you have chosen for yourself, in a personal or work setting. If you are told in your dream whether or not you have been successful in an interview, this may reflect how well you believe you are doing with a current undertaking or project. If you are very late for a dream interview or miss it completely, this may represent a fear that you have in some way missed the boat regarding a work opportunity, and that other similar chances will not appear again in the near future. Where in the dream interview you are required to give a presentation, consider your feelings about performing such a task. If you approached the presentation with relish, then perhaps you view yourself as a good communicator who gets their point across thoroughly. If you view the task with trepidation, you might be seeing yourself as a poor communicator, who doesn't explain themselves clearly enough. If you are the interviewer, you may be looking for the final piece of a puzzle you are currently trying to solve. Whom were you interviewing and how suitable for the post did they seem? If it was someone you know, how might they be able to help you with a current seemingly intractable problem?

MAKING A SPEECH

If you were making a speech in your dream, the content of this may have a direct bearing on what you see as being of utmost importance to you in your waking life. If you spoke passionately or with anger, this may be relevant to how you view a particular issue at the moment. If you feel fear when about to make the speech, perhaps there is something you need to convey to an individual or a group of people that you can't quite face up to. The way in which your speech was received is also interesting. If you were cheered or applauded, then you might be brimming with confidence about a current project, whereas jeers or boos indicate a sense of uncertainty or lack of self-confidence. If close friends or family members were in the audience to support you while you made your speech, you will probably be experiencing feelings of being appreciated or well supported by these groups. If you were watching someone else making a speech, was it someone known to you personally or perhaps a famous person? If it was a friend or colleague, were they saying anything that might be of relevance to your waking life? If the speech-maker was a famous person, this could either be a form of wish-fulfilment to meet them, or they may have a real interest in an issue which is of great concern to you.

LANGUAGE/CODE

In some dreams, you may find yourself being talked to in an unknown foreign or nonsensical language. Such dreams may tell of your concerns about missing the point with regard to an element of your working life. Perhaps you need something explained to you in more depth, or someone to take you through a task in a calm and measured way. If you are speaking a new language, perhaps this conveys a message for you to stretch your horizons. It could be time to face new challenges, or to embark upon an exciting adventure of some sort. If code is involved in your dream, this may imply either that you are failing to communicate clearly with someone, or that someone is failing to get through to you. Try to remember the code signs, and see if any of them mean anything significant in your waking life.

GUEST/VISITOR

Guests and visitors are frequent characters in dreams. Sometimes they are people known to us, whereas on other occasions they are complete strangers. If the visitor was known to you, how did they appear and what did they seem to be telling you? Maybe in your waking life, you are expecting some important news to reach you. Were they imparting simple information or divulging a secret? Were you pleased by their appearance or perturbed by it? If you were uneasy about the guest, then maybe you are concerned about an unwanted interference in your life or someone giving you too much advice. If you are the person who is doing the visiting, this may suggest that you are looking to broaden your horizons in a quest for new experiences. If the guest or visitor outstayed their welcome or proved very hard to get rid of, then think about your current social relationships. Are you maintaining certain friendships that are past their sell-by date? If, however, you were the guest whom people wanted to leave, then maybe you are not being sensitive enough toward other people in some sphere of your life. Think about what this might be, and if there are any steps you could take to make your presence felt a little less heavily.

BROKEN SPEECH/STAMMER

If in a dream you have problems speaking, or find yourself stammering, this may reveal a very real worry about your ability to communicate with others. Who was listening when you were speaking? Were they supportive or did they mock you? If the stammering is overcome easily, this can reveal that a current problem will be solved without too much effort. If, however, the speech problem persists, then you may be experiencing serious difficulties in getting your point across in a family or business situation.

INTERPRETER

If an interpreter appears in one of your dreams, this might symbolize the need you have for something to be translated for you. Perhaps a concept or definition in the workplace is not making sense to you, and you need some extra help to understand it. If you are the one doing the interpreting, then possibly someone close to you is relying on you too heavily in social situations, and their reliance is placing too much of a burden on your shoulders.

> "A good message will always find a messenger."
>
> AMELIA E. BARR

Natural Forces

NATURAL FORCES APPEARING IN DREAMS ARE OFTEN LINKED TO THE POWERFUL EMOTIONAL WORLD

OF THE DREAMER. STORMS, GALES, AND HURRICANES CAN INDICATE DEEP EMOTIONAL TURMOIL OR

STRIFE WHILE GENTLE RAIN OR A CALM BREEZE MAY SYMBOLIZE A TIME OF PEACE AND INNER

TRANQUILLITY IN THE DREAMER'S DAY-TO-DAY EXISTENCE.

FIRE

Dreams of fire are normally associated with the two themes of destroying and purifying or rebirth. Dream fires which are left untended and appear to be moving out of control might underpin the dreamer's anger or temper in their waking world. If a fire was put out, this can be a sign that the dreamer's emotional needs have not been allowed to be expressed. Where the dreamer stands or sits in relation to the fire can also be significant. If you are very close to the flames, this may indicate a nearness to an emotional situation. If you are running away from the fire or attempting to shield yourself from the flames, you could be wishing to protect yourself from a current delicate emotional situation. If the fire is a warm fire burning safely in a fireplace in a cosy room, this can tell of an inner sense of satisfaction or pleasure with one's lot in life. In many Eastern cultures, the dead are burnt, as an act of purging. Consider this association with fire and whether or not it bears any relevance to you. Perhaps some aspect of your life needs purging. A fire that grows gracefully, in a controlled manner, may represent the more spiritual side of your character, and could be a message for you to make a deeper connection with your own spirituality. Fires in dreams can also represent sexual passion or desire, and it is worth noting if there was another figure with you at the fireside. If you dream of a burning house or home, you may be feeling in need of some form of emotional cleansing. Traditionally when crops caught fire within a dream, interpreters claimed this as a symbol that a famine was approaching. In the modern world, burning crops have come to represent the possibility of hard times in the future. A dream fire engine might correspond with your need to protect someone close to you. It might also mean that you are the one seeking some form of protection. If you set fire to a property or object, this might reveal your feelings of anger toward an individual or organization. You should consider what it was you set alight, and how it made you feel?

WATER

Water is seen as a symbol of the emotional side of the dreamer's waking life, and, as water freezes and turns to ice, dreams about ice can be signs of the emotional freezing which people sometimes experience. Maybe you have been thinking of someone close to you in very harsh times recently, or feel that someone is judging you in an extremely cold manner. If, however, the ice in the dream is melting, this can indicate a thawing of personal relations, or the loosening of energies which have hitherto been frozen away. Ice dreams sometimes act as a message for the dreamer to stop procrastinating and get on with a proposed plan of action. Ice dreams are often seen as a symbol that the dreamer's creativity will be required at optimum levels in the near future. If you are walking uncomfortably on thin ice in a dream, this may reveal fears about your financial or work situation. Perhaps you have taken a big risk and are concerned about the consequences of such an action. Conversely, if the ice you walk on is thick and secure, you may be feeling content and satisfied with a recent decision you have made. If you were skating on ice with another person, you might be experienc-

ing some form of conflict in your relationship with this figure or indeed with
another person.

VOLCANO

Volcanic dreams can symbolize dramatic
changes in your life. To dream of a volcano, with its potential for explosive erup-
tion, might be a message for you to consider a radical shake-up in your waking
world. If the volcano is dormant and still,
this can indicate a time of quiet contempla-
tion. Perhaps you are considering moving
too quickly on a work project, and need to
step back and reconsider all of your
options. If the volcano is about to erupt,
this could be connected to a fear regarding
some authority figure in your world.
Perhaps you have done something which
you fear will lead to recriminations. If you
watched a volcano erupt from a distance,
you may be concerned about a sizeable
change in someone else's life. Maybe you
want to discuss this with them but have so
far not been able to. If you are very close to
the volcano when it erupts, you might be
feeling that hitherto suppressed emotions
are in need of exploding.

EARTHQUAKE

The earthquake dream is generally tied to
the very core of a person's life, as their personal earth is moving. On a positive level,
an earthquake dream might signify an
important change in your life, which although major and
disruptive, you are anticipating with excitement. However, if
the earthquake experience is traumatic, you may be dread-
ing some form of change which looms on the horizon.
Maybe you need to spend more time preparing for this
change in your waking life. If you see your own home being
shaken or destroyed by an earthquake, this can tell of personal fears concerning the home foundation of your life. Are
you worried that a relationship is in danger of crumbling, or
is there a practical or financial worry? If you witness a building toppling over because of a dream earthquake, you may
be feeling that you are carrying too much responsibility in
some sphere of your life at present.

OCEAN

The ocean or vast seas are usually linked to the unconscious.
Interpretation of ocean dreams is often connected to the
state of the water, and whether it was rough or calm. Some
analysts have argued that the ocean is a symbol of the mother, either a personal mother or Mother Earth. Many also add
that the ocean carries with it many feminine qualities such as
insight and intuition. A tranquil ocean is sometimes said to
represent peaceable relations with those close to you, in particular women friends and family members. If you are swept
away by towering ocean waves, you may be feeling that current emotional problems are starting to get out of hand.
If you are shipwrecked on an ocean, this might reveal your
fears of being emotionally or financially shipwrecked in life.
Maybe it is time to take an overview of a particular aspect of
your life which is troubling you. If there were several ships
on your dream ocean, this may represent a friendship
group. Try to recall if the ships were able to sail harmo-
niously over the waters or if they collided with one another.
If you were swimming in an ocean, this might represent

your desire to make a closer connection with your unconscious, and to discover more about your inner self.

SKY

Dream skies are often interpreted as a symbol of the heights to which the dreamer wishes to aspire in their waking life. If the sky is very clear, this may be a portent of satisfying or successful times in the future. It can also be a message that a present problem does have a clear solution. If the sky is cloudy, the dreamer may be concerned about difficult times around the corner. The dreamer's life may also be clouded in some way, and they need to move on if they are to see brighter days ahead. The sky can also symbolize creative energies and the untapped potential of the dreamer. If the sky is a very pure shade of blue, the dreamer may discover something which they had previously thought lost, while a sky of many colors may foretell of some traveling experience in the near future. If you dream you are actually flying, then it is possible that you are trying to attain an overview of a current problem.

SUN

Many dream interpreters link sun dreams to the heat of the dreamer's emotional state. The sun has also been historically linked with the ideas of truth and intellectual clarity. If the sun is especially bright without being blinding, this can indicate the emotional and intellectual strength of the dreamer. If the sun is hidden by clouds or is giving off a very weak light, the dreamer may be feeling emotionally drained at present. If you witness the rising of the sun in your dream, then new opportunities may be presenting themselves to you, either socially or in a work situation. A rising sun can also link to the dreamer's expectation of receiving some good news. If the dream sun is setting, this can refer to feelings of negativity or fear, and may underpin a belief that plans are not taking off as they should be, or potential is not being reached. If the sun is glaring red hot, this may link to feelings of anger which you hold in relation to a friend or family member. Try to recall how you protected yourself from the blazing sun. Did you wear sunglasses, or retreat into the shade of a building? If in your dream the sun shines directly onto your face creating a pleasant sensation, this could indicate a feeling of deep-rooted satisfaction with the way your life is unfolding.

STAR

Stars in dreams have often been associated with the dreamer's goals in life, particularly if these goals are challenging or adventurous. They may in fact represent unrealistic goals, and on waking the dreamer should assess how likely they are to make it to their intended destination. The proximity of the dreamer to the star may be a reflection of how far they are toward achieving a set aim, and the star may be able to act as a guiding light. If there is a clear sky which is full of glittering stars, this can reflect clarity of vision, or the possibility of financial success. It also may reflect the coming of a possible journey. If the stars are pale and their lights flicker sporadically, then hard times may be waiting ahead of the dreamer.

STORM

In dream interpretation, storms are often viewed as harbingers of turbulence or trying times. The severity of the storm can have significant ramifications for the interpretation of the dream. Being caught out in a storm can link to obstacles you are facing in your work life, or foretell of obstacles which may lie in your way if you attempt to be innovative in the workplace. If the storm is shortlived, your problems may peter out without too much trouble, whereas a long and raging storm can indicate a series of complicated problems. Storms in dreams, however, can also relate to the ending of a problematic period in your life—the calm after the storm. If you find shelter easily or if the storm blows out in the dream, you may be on the verge of finding a solution to a problem or difficult situation.

THUNDER

Dream thunder was interpreted in ancient times as the gods speaking to the dreamer, often in a harsh and condemnatory fashion. At times the criticism will be clearly understood from the other symbols in the dream, but at others it will not be clear what the wrath of the gods was directed at. If a person appears within the thunder scenario, this may well be a figure against whom you are harboring negative feelings, or who is in some way displeased with you.

Thunder may also represent a message from your unconscious, warning you about some aspect of your life. Thunder can also represent an authority figure in your life, perhaps a parent, boss, or former teacher. Try to figure out if there is anything you are feeling especially guilty about, and work out if the guilt is justified or an unnecessary waste of time and energy. Thunder in your dream which takes place over your home suggests a concern about finances or damage to your possessions, while distant thunder may signify that certain people who you are close to are not what they seem.

LIGHTNING

Dream lightning can symbolize the flash of a great new idea or inspiration. If there is one bolt of lightning, a clear and focused idea may be on the verge of being developed. If there are many flashes of lightning, you may have to be selective about which inspirational ideas you choose to pursue. Dream lightning is also connected to the idea of power and illumination. Are you seeking guidance from someone relating to an issue you have yet to fathom, or are you required to shed light on a situation for a friend or colleague? If the latter is the case, do you feel under pressure to provide this explanation to another or are you content to be of service?

RAIN

Rain, with its water associations, is usually linked to the dreamer's emotional state. If the rain is pouring down and shows no sign of abating, then you may be feeling inundated with emotional troubles, and in need of a change of scene. If it is drizzling gently, your present emotional state may be quite calm and balanced. If you are told that it will rain, and then no rain is forthcoming, potential hurdles in your social or work life may never materialize.

Animal Kingdom

THE ANIMAL KINGDOM FREQUENTLY APPEARS IN OUR DREAMS UNDER DIFFERENT GUISES, AND THE MEANINGS AND INTERPRETATIONS ATTRIBUTED TO DREAM ANIMALS ARE VARIED. IN SOME INSTANCES DREAM ANIMALS ARE SAID TO REPRESENT FIGURES OF AUTHORITY SUCH AS PARENTS, BOSSES OR TEACHERS. IN OTHER INSTANCES A PARTICULAR ANIMAL MAY BE SYMBOLIC OF SOME PRIMITIVE PART OF OUR PSYCHE, REPRESENTING REPRESSED EMOTIONS OR FEARS OF UNTAMED BEASTS THAT LIE BELOW THE SURFACE. A DANGEROUS OR THREATENING ANIMAL MAY BE A SIGN OF REPRESSED RAGE AND ANGER THAT MAY NEED TO BE ADDRESSED. A WOUNDED ANIMAL, HOWEVER, MAY BE CALLING YOU TO NURTURE SOME ASPECT OF YOURSELF. TO GET THE MOST HELPFUL INTERPRETATION FROM YOUR ANIMAL DREAMS IT IS IMPORTANT TO REFLECT ON YOUR OWN PERSON-AL ASSOCIATIONS WITH THAT ANIMAL AND HOW IT IMPACTS ON YOUR WORLD.

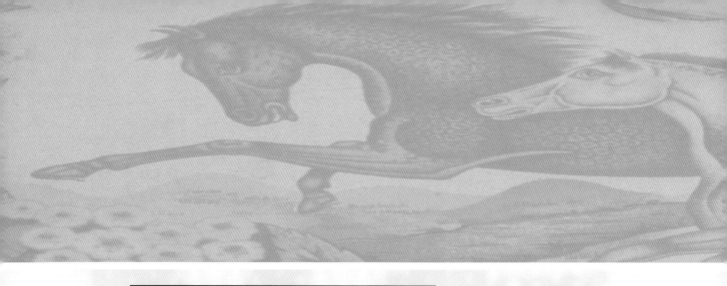

LIONS

The lion as king of the jungle is often associated with notions of power, protectiveness, and territory. The lion as zodiac sign is connected to leadership, strength, and fire. If your dream lion seems to be protecting something, it may be telling of your need to keep some information or aspect of your psyche safe and secure. You may be feeling threatened in some way. A sleeping lion suggests that all is well and that you are comfortable with life. Women who dream of lions may be connecting with their animus—the male side of their psyche. A cowardly lion reminiscent of the one in *The Wizard of Oz* may be a sign that the dreamer desires or needs to gather some courage to fight oncoming battles.

DOGS

The animal or instinctive part of your nature is often represented by dream dogs. If the dog is vicious and attacking it may be telling you of hidden anger that lies within your psyche and you may be repressing your inner desire to lash out at someone. Dogs can also represent feelings of loyalty and faithfulness—a man's best friend. Your dream dog may represent someone you trust or feel close to or it may represent yourself as loyal friend to another. It is useful to recognize what other dream characters were present in the dream and how they interacted with the dog to give you further clues to your dream meanings.

CATS

As with most dreams, your interpretation of cat dreams will depend largely on your association with the animal. Cats broadly represent notions of the feminine. If you are scared of cats, then you may be frightened of the feminine aspects of your personality. A black cat in a dream can be connected with good luck. Black cats are also connected with witches, so the

meaning they may have for you will be linked to your beliefs about witches. Do you see them as evil and frightening or as good women who represent the powers of spirituality and psychic strength? Cats' eyes can tell of vision and insight in the dreamers world.

MICE

Dreams of mice will depend on your own associations with them, but can often be connected to notions of speed, smallness, agility, and survival. If a mouse appears in your dream, try to notice how it looked. Was it timid and frightened? Was the mouse sleepy like the dormouse in *Alice in Wonderland*? Was it cute like Jerry who always outsmarts Tom the cat? Do you have some longing to be quick-witted or do you feel more of a timid person inside?

ELEPHANTS

Elephants never forget. They are strong, yet generally do not attack. They represent power and majesty, but can sometimes be humiliated like the circus elephant Dumbo. Indian elephants can tell of things regal and respectful. If the elephant has tusks, what are your thoughts about the rarity of ivory? All these may offer tell-tale signs to assist you in understanding your dream.

SHEEP

Sheep may symbolize passivity or conformity. Perhaps you feel that you are being easily

led and the dream of a sheep may warn you of your need to regain some element of control in your life. Like lambs to the slaughter, your dream may tell of some impending doom that awaits you and you may need to leave the herd and go astray. Dreams of black sheep can represent feelings of exclusion and difference—the black sheep of the family. Some dream analysts say that black sheep indicate feelings of temptation, envy or greed.

BIRDS

Soaring birds often represent freedom, flight, and escape. Perhaps you yearn to escape the humdrum nature of life or there is some aspect of your unconscious that needs to be set free to fly. Traditionally birds have been linked with the spirit world. The shaman is said to fly to make contact with the spirit world, and a dream symbol of a bird may suggest balance and wholeness within the psyche. Similarly birds can be seen as messengers bringing news from other worlds. If the bird is flying toward you in the dream, you may wish to take heed of what your subconscious is telling you. Carrion birds such as ravens and crows are connected to death. This does not mean that they predict an imminent death, but may express your inner worry about the death of someone close or even your own death.

To dream of a parrot may warn of a superficial side to your character. Perhaps you are unsure of what you believe and are just mimicking those around you. Peacock dreams tell of sexuality and pride. You may even be feeling quite ostentatious and strut around displaying your plumage. Swans usually tell of feelings of beauty and elegance. Remember the story of the ugly duckling, though. Underneath that beautiful exterior lay a lonely little creature that never really belonged anywhere. The dove is a bird of peace and any dream that features it may tell of a yearning for peace. This may mean an inner harmony connected to your unconscious mind or it may refer to peace between family, friends or even political peace. Try to listen to your dream to find out your own individual meaning. The eagle is usually a majestic and powerful symbol of pride and majesty. Any dream that features an eagle may be connected to beliefs about your own inner strength and beauty or that of someone close to you. Flocks of birds that appear are likely to tell of your desire to be part of the crowd or perhaps your yearning to escape from it. Notice how you were feeling on waking from the dream. Were you elated to see or be flying with the masses? Or did you long to see them divide and find some individuality?

FISH

Fish, according to Jung, represent the deepest levels of the unconscious. He suggested that this was due to their cold-bloodedness and their ancient evolution from the start of the universe. Fish dreams therefore can be indicators of deep-rooted fears and anxieties that are far from being uncovered in waking life. Some interpreters say that fish symbolize aspects of fertility or that good fruitful times lie ahead. Dead fish are said to represent disappointments or failures. Fish are also said to represent greed or libido. Given all these possible interpretations, it is worth focusing on the fish in your dream to ascertain the personal meaning it holds for you.

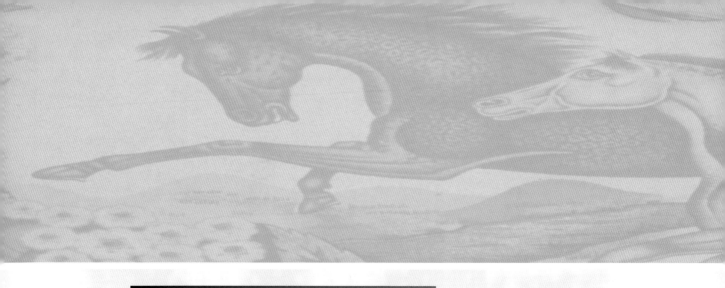

BOARS

The boar in your dream may be wild and untamed and there-fore represent an untamed aspect of your psyche that may need reining in. If the boar is aggressive and ferocious, it is important not to be frightened of it but try to listen to what this dream message is telling you. You may want to try speaking with the boar to find out what he wants. Some analysts suggest that a wild boar may be traced back to an Oedipal conflict where the male infant's desire for his mother and rivalry with his father create feelings of rage and guilt, and for the female her longing for her father results in similar anguish directed toward her mother or turned in on herself.

SNAKES

Snakes are often said to symbolize power, sexuality, and intu-itive wisdom. In the Judeo-Christian tradition they are associ-ated with evil and deception, as illustrated in the Garden of Eden when the serpent tricked Eve into eating the forbidden fruit. However, in other traditions the snake is said to symbol-ize rejuvenation and healing in its ability to slough off one skin and grow another. It is the emblem of the Greco-Roman god of medicine. The snake depicted with its tail in its mouth is an ancient symbol of the cycle of life, death, and rebirth. To dream of attacking a snake or killing a snake may be associat-ed to the dreamer overcoming people around you who wish to see you fail. Snake dreams also signify deep-rooted jealousy.

HORSES

Horses are traditionally associated with power, majesty, and sexuality. For example, a dream of mounting a horse may rep-resent some kind of sexual act. On a wider level horses tend to symbolize aspects of our sensuality and animal instincts. Some analysts suggest that dream horses tell of unconscious emo-tions or unexpressed feelings that we may be harboring. If the horse in the dream is tightly tethered, this may be a sign for you to unleash some inner feelings and let yourself go in some way. However, if your dream horse is galloping away at breakneck speed, you may be wish-ing to escape or yearning to break free from the chains of everyday life. Dreams of black horses are often connected with death and funerals. Although this is unlikely to be liter-al death, it may highlight an aspect of your inner self or your world that you are losing or that may be withering away and could need some attention.

HOUSEHOLD PETS

If the animal that appears in your dream is actually a domestic pet, whether it is a cat, a dog or something more unusual, you may need to consider your feelings in your wak-ing life about this animal. The pet in the dream may represent an aspect of your own personality that you instinctively feel needs to come out at this point or perhaps it needs to be tamed. Try to work out your waking associations to the pet and your feelings toward in order to best understand the mes-sage that lies within.

MONKEYS AND CHIMPANZEES

Monkeys are usually connected to ideas of mischief and trouble-making. Some part of your own psyche may be up to mischief and you might even be trying to catch yourself out or trip yourself up in some way. It may

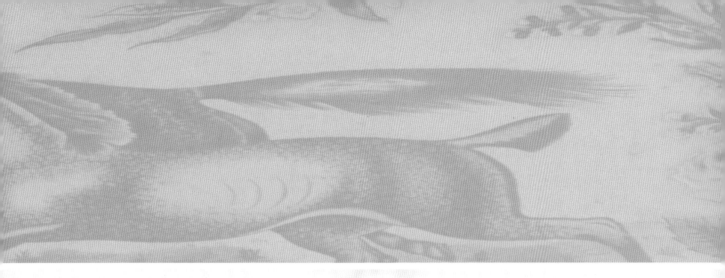

be worth taking stock to help yourself out before the impudent part of yourself gets you into trouble. Monkeys are also associated with sex and sexuality—so think about how that might be developing too.

INSECTS

Ants are associated with industry and hard work, so to dream of ants may be linked to your conscious or unconscious thoughts about work of some kind. This may not necessarily be connected to the workplace itself, but may be connected to work within the home. Perhaps you feel that people around you aren't pulling their weight or maybe you feel that you would like to reduce your workload in some way.

Caterpillar and butterfly dreams more often than not represent an inner longing for change. Think laterally about this. The change may not be practical, but the dream may be telling of your desire to change some aspect of your personality or the way you interact with your world. If you dream of moths, however, you may need to be careful. Moths slowly eat away at clothes and before you know it they have destroyed a garment without you even noticing. Take care of precious aspects of yourself or those around you, because there may be some destructive force that you are failing to recognize and things may not be all they seem.

Scorpion dreams are usually quite concrete in their symbolism. The scorpion with the sting in its tale can be a killer. As with the moth, a dream of a scorpion portends potentially dangerous people or times ahead. The difficulty lies in spotting where the danger lies, as it can creep up on you. Take care not to be fooled by those who seem close, as they may be on the attack.

WOLF

The wild and aggressive wolf that appears in our dreams is more often than not connected with our inner animalistic aggressiveness and may tell of personal fears about this dangerous and destructive aspect of our own psyche. As with other animal dreams, the wolf dream does have strong connections with unconscious and conscious ideas about sexuality. For a woman it may mean that she finds an aspect of men and male sexuality highly threatening. The image of the wolf as deceptive and sly may tell that you are feeling vulnerable right now and you perceive something or someone around you as dishonest and dangerous. If your dream wolf bites you this suggests that harm may come to a friend or adversary, while pack of wolves running together signifies a fear of being robbed.

FROG

The frog in Western European mythology has connections with the fairy tale about the frog and the prince. In this story a young princess is visited in bed by a frog on a nightly basis. The girl finds the frog disgusting, but over time she grows to love him and when she finally kisses him he turns into a handsome prince. Some analysts suggest that this story and dreams of this nature indicate overcoming sexual fear. Others suggest that the fable shows how the unconscious is integrated into waking life. At first it can feel disgusting, but over time it can be beautiful and feel good. If a frog appears in your dream, it may be worth considering what role it played and your own personal associations to frogs in general.

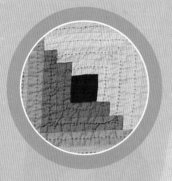

Colors

MANY PEOPLE CLAIM THAT THEY ONLY EVER DREAM IN BLACK AND WHITE. OTHERS ARE ABLE TO

IDENTIFY SHADES AND TONES OF COLOR IN THEIR DREAMS. FOR THOSE WHO DO DREAM IN COLOR,

THE TEXTURE AND TONE OF THE ADDED SHADES MAKE DREAMS AT TIMES SEEM MORE ALIVE. THOSE

WHO DO DREAM IN COLOR MAY BE MORE AWARE OF THEIR VISUAL ENVIRONMENT AND THEY CAN

HARNESS THIS POTENTIAL TO UNDERSTAND THEIR DREAM MEANINGS. WHEN DREAMING IN COLOR IT

IS IMPORTANT TO TRY TO REMEMBER IF THE COLORS WERE BRIGHT AND VIVID, OR MUTED AND

FADED. THE STRENGTH OF THE COLORS MAY BE LINKED DIRECTLY TO YOUR EMOTIONS AND

EMOTIONAL NEEDS AT THE TIME OF THE DREAM. RICH, CLEAR COLORS MAY SIGNIFY INNER

STRENGTH OR A SENSE OF WELL-BEING, WHEREAS WEAK COLORS CAN REPRESENT FEELINGS OF BEING

JADED OR WASHED OUT IN SOME WAY.

BLACK

Black is viewed as a representation of death and mourning in many cultures, and its appearance in dreams can be linked to emotions of sadness or grief. It has also been linked to notions of passivity. However, in other cultures, black is seen as portraying confidence and messages of hope, and some writers have tied black to the idea of Mother Earth. Some dream analysts point to the shadowy effects of black in dreams, and claim these are symbols of the dreamer's "shadow" or unfulfilled part of their life. A black funeral procession in a dream may signify concerns about difficulties in the dreamer's life which loom on the horizon. A black coffin can represent a friendship that is heading toward extinction. Such a dream may force the dreamer to reevaluate the status of this friendship. A magpie can symbolize the need for a new approach to a relationship or work issue—the dreamer's current approach may be doomed to failure. A dream blackbird is often cited as a precursor for the dreamer to show great courage in the future. Black sheep which appear in dreams are usually associated with notions of envy or temptation. A night dream scene that is shrouded in blackness may relate to a certain lack of direction in one or more spheres of the dreamer's waking life. Blackberries are seen as a symbol of setbacks. This is connected with an ancient superstition which denoted blackberries as food for the Devil.

WHITE

White is associated with purity and innocence in Western cultures, perhaps best represented by the virginal bride. However, in the East, white is associated with dying, grief, and mourning. Within the Western context, therefore, dreams involving white can be representations of pure emotions on the part of the dreamer. A white sky is often interpreted as a form of wishful thinking, perhaps for a purer, more simple life. A white room may symbolize a state of calm or a sense that the dreamer is at peace with themselves. A forest covered in white trees could be connected to a deep-rooted wish to embark on a new and positive project or undertaking. The dove is well-known as a political symbol of peace, but appearing within a dream, it may signify a wish for an end to some personal conflict or unfinished business. A white book appearing in your dream may be a symbol of stable foundations, so it is worth considering if you are laying foundations currently for a personal or professional experience. A white hand may relate to the blossoming of a new relationship. A white room may be connected to feelings of personal tranquillity. A white podium or stage can be a sign that the dreamer will enjoy some success in a public arena in the future. White water is linked to notions of emotional purity, and may suggest that the dreamer is in need of cleansing some part of their emotional life.

Dream scene
Jane reported that she had the same dream on a regular basis when her second marriage was approaching. In the dream she is walking through an art gallery and every painting and sculpture in the gallery is white. In addition the chairs, sofas, tables, and computers in the research library are also white. This contrasts with Jane's own dream clothes, which are a multicolor splash. On waking from the dream, Jane stated that she always felt a sense of some-

how not being prepared. When she looked more closely at the feelings and emotions surrounding the dream, she realized that the white gallery was tied up with her childhood notions of the purity of marriage and represented her feelings of guilt at entering this covenant for a second time. Her colorful clothing symbolized the more adventurous and forward-thinking aspects of her personality. Thus the meeting of the pure white and the mix of colors symbolized her own moral and spiritual conflict regarding the breakup of her first marriage and the advent of her second marriage.

BLUE

Blue historically bears associations with ideas of spirituality and transparency. Within the sphere of dreams, blue is often taken as a symbol of the conscious mind, especially in dreams of blue skies. The many shades of blue can have an influence on the interpretation of the dream. A shimmering bright blue may reveal feelings of tranquillity or well-being, while a dark angry blue can suggest feelings of loneliness or isolation. Clear blue dream water is often interpreted as a sign that the dreamer should sit up and take notice of their emotional state and emotional needs. The appearance of a blue precious stone in a dream may be a portent of liberation from a particular aspect of your life with which you are currently dissatisfied. Blue clothes are often linked to notions of masculinity or the male part of the dreamer's psyche. Blue birds are said to represent feelings of hope, forward-thinking, and emotions connected with freedom. Blue smoke may be connected to a new and exciting project, but try to remember if the smoke obscured your view, and if so how did this make you feel? A blue vase may be a sign that the dreamer is in a present state of emotional containment.

GREEN

In dream interpretation, green is often viewed as a symbol of growth or flourishing development. On the positive side, green is linked to feelings of calm and hope, whereas negatively green is linked to jealousy. A dream greenhouse may be a sign that hard work and cultivation will produce a bumper harvest in some part of your personal or professional life. A green field could relate to inner feelings of calm with the world around you. Green fruits tend to signify that a current project is not yet ripe and that patience is required until the time is right to begin. Green vegetables can be tied to the idea of personal health or growth, and may symbolize feelings of well-being. Green eyes have traditionally been linked to feelings of envy or jealousy. Try to recall if the eyes were your own or someone else's. This may be relevant in ascertaining if there are feelings of jealousy around yourself. A green path or pathway might be linked to a physical or emotional journey which will take up a considerable period of time. Green moss is at times said to represent feelings of inner peace and security.

RED

Red in life is associated with fire, heat, blood, and passion. In dreams, these fiery themes are often mirrored and dreams in red are seen to be connected with passion, energy or vitality. Red also has connotations of anger and rage, toward either a person, group or situation. It also has connotations with dan-

ger and prohibition. It is worth taking time to consider the message of the color red in your dream and the tone that was being conveyed. A red heart may uncover deep-seated sexual energy or desire, possibly connected to real feelings in one's waking life. Red ears may be signifiers of embarrassment or guilt. A red nose is often taken as a symbol of an inquisitive nature. Perhaps there is a fact or figure you are desperate to uncover, but as yet haven't discovered how. Red flames are believed to imply the threat of danger, and it is worth thinking about one's own situation and fears following such a dream. Red wine can be linked to feelings of satisfaction or happiness. It may also be a symbol of financial satisfaction. Within the Hindu tradition, a bride wearing a red wedding dress can be interpreted as a symbol of life itself. A red rose is often tied to the idea of romance and seduction. Who was holding the red rose in your dream, and was it being offered as a token of love?

YELLOW

Many dream interpreters see yellow as a symbol of the dreamer's intellectual capacity and their ability to think in clear and logical ways. Therefore, when a dream is yellow in some form, this may signify the exercising of the dreamer's thought processes and may underpin the fact that they are thinking very clearly in some arena of their life. In traditional terms, yellow is associated with cowardice. A dream of a bright yellow sun can symbolize inner energy. A yellow dream bird may be tied to notions of a desire to be free from some aspect of one's life. A banana can be a direct link to the need for extra sustenance in the form of a physical or spiritual energy boost. Yellow flowers are usually linked to creativity and the possibility of a creative change. Firing yellow arrows from a bow could indicate that with the power of incisive thinking you will attain the goals you have set yourself. Yellow food in dreams is often connected with deep-seated feelings of fear or cowardice.

ORANGE

Orange has many associations, especially with generosity, optimism, and nobility. It is generally viewed as a warm color, connected with sunshine and brightness. Dreams in which orange appears are often taken as signs of positive change within the dreamer's real life. However, some dream analysts point out that orange also has links with mistrust, and thus the dreamer should be wary of feelings of uncertainty or doubt. An orange map can be taken as a sign that a possible travel adventure is well worth the trip. Orange soil represents a positive journey, perhaps in connection with one's work. An orange elevator may signify an upturn in the dreamer's emotional state following a state of flux or an emotional low. An orange hat can signify a creative spark, potentially the beginning of an innovative idea or plan. A flower which is orange may symbolize a sense of contentment with one's own life situation. An orange arm or clenched fist can signify emotions of anger, hostility or aggression. A sour orange, in spite of its bitter taste, may represent a sign of emotional stability or happiness.

PURPLE

Purple is traditionally associated with majesty, authority, and the legal profession. In the West, purple robes and gowns are worn by Royalty and those in positions of power. Purple in dreams is thus associated

with loyalty, authority, and justice. A purple bird in a dream may be connected to the idea of personal pride and dignity. The dream interpretation depends on the stature of the bird. Was it preening its feathers, or lying low in shame? Purple fish have been associated with the notion of spirituality. A purple cheetah could be a symbol of your deepest emotions, and it's important to remember exactly what the cheetah was doing in the dream to aid the interpretation. A purple camel can be taken as a sign that the dreamer is feeling subservient to some authority figure or institution in their life. It may mean that certain orthodoxies need to be challenged. A procession of people all dressed in purple may be a portent of some ceremony that will take place in your future. People with purple complexions can be signs of social gatherings, either ones that have taken place, or ones that are still at the planning stages. A purple pen could indicate the need for more openness and honesty in your communicating with others.

PINK

Pink has many connections to ideas of love, especially love that is unconditional. Some dream interpreters also link the color with the human soul's great powers of healing, or with the heart Chakra (the center of spiritual or psychic energy). A pink window can symbolize an existing opportunity which has been noted but not yet explored. Pink clothes are usually taken as signs that the dreamer wishes in some way to be wrapped in love by someone who is close to them. Pink flowers are often associated with a desirable social outcome or the joys of future social happenings. Pink steps may mean that a task will be achieved, only after a considerable amount of hard work. A pink face can be a symbol of emotional openness. It may be a portent that you will reveal some of your deepest emotions to someone you trust. A pink heart could be linked to yearnings for someone who is somewhere far away. A pink cupboard can be related to the idea that you are storing love for someone, perhaps waiting until you find the right occasion to reveal your innermost feelings to them.

GOLD

To dream of the color gold is often connected with wealth, jewels, and divinity. Some say that gold dreams are linked to growth, maturity and aging. It is helpful to notice what was colored gold in your dream. Was everything in gold or was there just one precious gold item? Were you able to touch and see the gold or was it out of your reach? The whole dream scenario will help you to locate the meaning. Perhaps there was some element of wishful thinking or gold digging, maybe even a degree of envy about someone else's wealth.

SILVER

Silver dreams have a slightly different meaning from those which occur in gold. They may often tell of luck, skill, and youth. In some cases to dream in silver may tell the dreamer of some ambition, aspiration or integrity. Notice the type and nature of silver in the dream. When polished, for example, silver takes on the role of a mirror and you may be able to see your reflection. If this is the case, your dream may be inviting you to take a step back and reflect on your mental, physical, and practical state of being.

Numbers & Time

NUMBERS AND SYMBOLS ASSOCIATED WITH TIME FREQUENT MANY OF OUR DREAMS. IN SOME INSTANCES THEIR APPEARANCE HAS A STRAIGHTFORWARD RELATION TO THE PASSING OF TIME— PERHAPS WE ARE FEELING THAT TIME IS PASSING TOO SLOWLY, TOO QUICKLY, OR MAYBE EVEN AT THE DESIRED PACE. DAYS AND WEEKS, MONTHS AND YEARS ALL APPEAR IN DREAMS, AND THEIR SIGNIFICANCE IS SOMETIMES ONLY POSSIBLE TO INTERPRET IF THEY APPEAR ALONGSIDE A PARTICULAR NUMBER. SOMETIMES NUMERALS THEMSELVES APPEAR IN DREAMS, BUT AT OTHER TIMES NUMBERS ARE SYMBOLIZED BY GROUPS OR COLLECTIONS OF THINGS OR PEOPLE, AND IT CAN BE IMPORTANT TO REMEMBER HOW MANY ITEMS OR INDIVIDUALS THERE WERE IN A PARTICULAR DREAM SCENE.

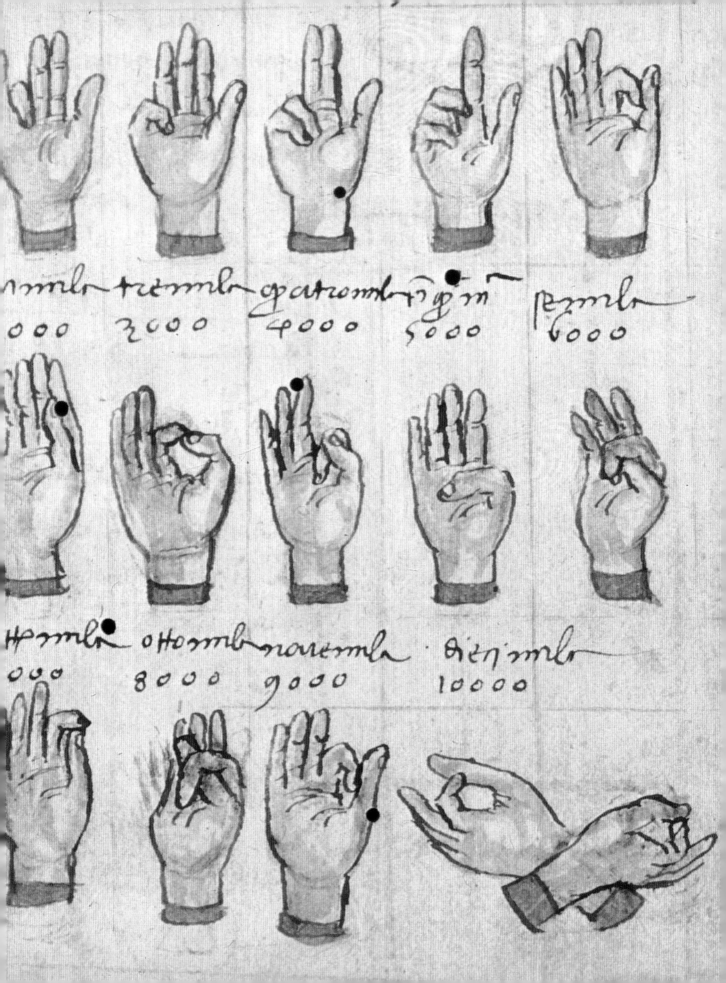

nmla   tremlra   oparonmbrī g m̄   ẛemlra
000   2000   4000   6000
                                         5000

Hemlra   ottomb   nonemla   dieṇ imla
000   8000   9000   10000

ZERO

Theorists have attributed several meanings to the figure 0. For some, it is a sign of a new beginning, a "ground zero" for a project in hand. To these theorists, zero is untarnished by any particular numerical significance and is therefore an optimistic sign. For others, zero symbolizes a sense of dissatisfaction—the dreamer in some way feels like a nothing. They are aspiring to greater things, but can't seem to make it off the starting blocks. It has also been said that zero can relate to a sense of completion, relating to some aspect of the dreamer's life where nothing needs to be done or added. In this sense zero means balance and wholeness.

dream exercise

When you wake up, immediately try to catch your dream either by writing it down or recording it into a tape machine for later transcription. Notice everything about your dream. As well as the events and mood of the dream, try to pay attention to the numbers of people or objects within the dream. If there was a repeated action, notice how many times this action was carried out. If there were various objects in the dream, try to count them and link this to any possible interpretation. Later in the day, come back to your dream and use your notes to consider the meaning and interpretation of the dream and how it may help you in your waking life.

ONE

The number one has traditionally been connected to notions of unity and assurance. If the number one appears in your dream, it may be that you are feeling complete in some aspect of your life. Some analysts suggest that the number one is associated with communication skills and flexibility. The number one may be a direct reference to the self, the I or ego. If a one does appear, it is worth considering what views you are strongly holding at the time. Are these perspectives rational and fair, or have you per-

haps been hasty in making a judgment? It may also act as a sign that you need to improve your communication skills.

TWO

The number two has been given several meanings. It can represent ideas about symmetry, and balance. Yet for some, it has an underpinning of conflict between the dreamer and another, or perhaps between two different sections of the dreamer's psychological makeup. Following a dream in which two appears, it is important to ascertain whether an internal struggle is in need of resolution or whether the dream reflects current feelings of balance and symmetry. Two has also been seen as a representation of union, either between two people or between the unconscious and conscious. Some dream interpreters have also stated that it may signify a link between the feminine and masculine parts of the personality. In addition, several thinkers have tied the number to a desire to always be right. If this is the case, then the dreamer should be wary of coming into conflict with others if they aren't prepared to suffer fools gladly. The appearance of a two-faced figure may be of some significance if the figure is someone known to you. If this is the case, then it may suggest that you hold an underlying mistrust of this person. A two-faced figure may also represent two parts of yourself, possibly from your conscious and unconscious minds, which are in some way in conflict with one another.

THREE

In the Christian tradition the number three is connected to ideas about the Holy Trinity—Father, Child, and the Holy Ghost. Other triangles are mother, father, child and mind, body and spirit. If there are triangles in your waking life, your dream of the number three may tell of a need to stop yourself from being caught in the middle. Jung claimed that dreams involving the number three are connected to the notion that a task is well on the way to fruition but isn't completely ready. He claimed that the finishing piece to the puzzle may lie in untapping a section of your unconscious mind which is perhaps too daunting to tackle in waking life. Other dream analysts take a different perspective and state that three reveals a sense of something that is being completed. They see it as a number imbued with a sense of self-fulfilment. For certain theorists, three has symbolized uncertainty. They state that a dream involving the number three may be a call for one to approach a subject or person with a great deal of sensitivity and tactfulness.

FOUR

Four has often been associated with the idea of force, and in Jung's arguments, the number relates to the four human conscious forces of thinking, intuition, feeling, and sensation. Jung claimed that some of these forces are not properly developed, and therefore remain in the unconscious sphere of the dreamer's wak-

ing world. For the dreamer to achieve some sense of personal fulfilment, these undeveloped forces need to be moved into the conscious realm. Many other dream interpreters have written that four is a symbol of wholeness, linking the number to dramatic notions such as the four corners of the earth, the four elements or the four seasons. Christian thinkers have pointed to the four points of the cross as a symbol that the number is connected to wholeness. However, when the number four does appear in a dream, this may not be a symbol that the dreamer's life is complete, but may in fact be suggesting that certain steps are needed to achieve completeness. Four has also been said to have connotations of passion and envy. As an even number it encompasses a reasonable balance between emotion and sensation.

FIVE

In folklore, the number five is taken as a symbol of intellectuality. It has also been linked to the ideas of fairness and justice. Many interpreters see five as a portent of good luck and a positive number. In other traditions five represents the human pentagram that encompasses the whole of mankind. So if the number five appears in your dream take heed, the message may be of great magnitude.

SIX

The number six is usually associated with stable emotions, particularly those of a sensual nature. It was often customary to use it at wedding ceremonies and celebrated as a number of everlasting kinship. Some have claimed that six is a manifestation of completeness. In modern myth, the number has taken on sinister overtones with the idea that 666 is the number of the Devil.

SEVEN

Seven has been portrayed as a sign of possible completeness, but has also been earmarked as a sign that the dreamer may be seek-

ing a major change in their life. In addition, seven has been linked to the notions of freedom and honesty. Seven is a mystical number in the Jewish tradition. In the Old Testament there is talk of the farmers who would leave their land fallow every seventh year in order to give back to the earth. A Jewish bride will walk around her groom seven times. There are seven days of the week. "God blessed the seventh day" (Genesis 2: 3). If you dream of the number seven, perhaps your subconscious is urging you to take time out and replenish yourself and your spirit in some way.

EIGHT

Eight has strong traditional links to the ideas of hard work and gritty determination. It has also been connected to patience and the idea that practical contributions in the dreamer's life may reap the best rewards.

NINE

Nine has often been interpreted as a number connected to ideas of independence or originality. Many have seen it as a positive or forward-thinking number. However, others have remarked on its less than perfect qualities, as a score of nine out of ten always points to what could have been.

TEN

Ten with its two digits and even number status, is sometimes portrayed as a signifier of balance. If this number does appear in your dream, question the equilibrium in your life. Are you feeling balanced in home and work life, or is the dream a call to add some equilibrium into the manner in which you are living?

NEGATIVE NUMBERS

Negative or minus numbers do appear in dreams, but they are not necessarily negative symbols. In some instances, they may contain a message to the dreamer to step back from a current sit-

uation and evaluate it with more objectivity. Negative numbers may also be a reminder to take a few steps back from a current project, and revisit things that you thought were totally failsafe; glitches may still need to be ironed out. On the other hand, negative numbers may reveal a sense of negativity, and therefore represent a wake-up call for the dreamer to start taking positive steps toward change.

CLOCK OR WATCH

The appearance of a timepiece in your dream may have very significant connections to the way in which you allocate time in your life. It is important to remember how you felt during and after the dream. Was the pace of the timepiece indicative of your good time-management skills or was it telling you to speed up or slow down? Were the hands whirring in a frenzied motion or were they taking an age to move? The type of clock or watch can also be important. Was the timepiece a modern device, possibly with a plethora of functions? Or was it an old-fashioned grandfather clock? Such dreams may also reveal a sense that the dreamer is overly reliant on time. Are you too busy studying every clock you happen to see, instead of experiencing and enjoying your life as it happens?

SUNDIAL

The ancient appearance and workings of a sundial may suggest that there is an aspect of your life that has become outdated. Think

about this carefully and decide whether or not some aspect of the way you live or work is in need of modernization. In direct contrast to this interpretation, some have suggested that sundials represent a more simple and purer way of life without the interference of modern contraptions. In this scenario, their place in a dream could relate to the dreamer's yearning for a life less cluttered with gadgetry.

CALENDAR

This is a relatively common dream symbol and may be a reference to your life in the past or possibly the future. Was a particular year or date showing on the calendar, which could be tied to an event or issue you need to explore further? Was the calendar obscured in some way, preventing you from seeing an exact date or series of dates? Possibly, a calendar dream relates to the speedy passage of time, and may simply act as a message for you to take stock of a current situation, and not let the calendar of time get the better of you.

BEING EARLY OR LATE

Being early or late for appointments or meetings in dreams may be of significance for your waking life. If early, you should ask yourself if you are over-worried or over-planned in some aspect of your professional or personal life. If late, it should be considered if you are worried about missing the boat or being the last one to find out about something that is important.

TIME TRAVEL

If traveling to the past, it is important to remember if you traveled to an age within your lifetime or to an era before you were born. Traveling in the past can be linked to a desire to connect with an incident or situation in your childhood or youth which remains unresolved. Traveling into the future can indicate an impatience to achieve your goals, and to discover exactly what's going to happen to one of your projects. It can also highlight an optimism on the part of the dreamer, who awaits the future with some anticipation. However, if the future scenario was bleak and unwelcoming, then this can be a direct representation of the dreamer's fears concerning their personal or the world's future.

HISTORICAL PEOPLE AND EVENTS

It is not uncommon to have a dream in which you travel to a particular event of national or world historical importance or come face to face with a famous historical figure. These dreams are sometimes simple reflections of your interest in a particular time period or with a particular character, but they may be of deeper significance. For instance, if one becomes embroiled in a war scenario, this may be related to some personal conflict which is very much to the fore at present. A historical figure with negative connotations may be a symbol of someone close to you, for example a friend with whom you are experiencing problems or a work colleague who is proving difficult at the moment.

AGEING DREAMS

In some dreams, the dreamer or someone close to them appears to age rapidly in a very short space of time, sometimes becoming an extremely elderly person. To some, this process can be quite disconcerting or even frightening, as they witness the profound physical changes taking place. To others, such a dream may be of some comfort, perhaps indicating that the ageing process need not necessarily be a negative experience.

picture credits

index